easy to make!
Pasta, Rice & Noodles

Good Housekeeping

easy to make!
Pasta, Rice
& Noodles

COLLINS & BROWN

First published in Great Britain in 2009
by Collins & Brown
10 Southcombe Street
London W14 0RA

An imprint of Anova Books Company Ltd

The Good Housekeeping website is
www.allaboutyou.com/goodhousekeeping

10 9 8 7 6 5 4 3 2 1

ISBN 978-1-84340-499-6

A catalogue record for this book is available from the British
Library.

Reproduction by Dot Gradations Ltd
Printed and bound by Times Offset, Malaysia

This book can be ordered direct from the publisher. Contact the
marketing department, but try your bookshop first.

www.anovabooks.com

NOTES

- Both metric and imperial measures are given for the recipes. Follow either set of measures, not a mixture of both, as they are not interchangeable.
- All spoon measures are level.
  1 tsp = 5ml spoon; 1 tbsp = 15ml spoon.
- Ovens and grills must be preheated to the specified temperature.
- Use sea salt and freshly ground black pepper unless otherwise suggested.
- Fresh herbs should be used unless dried herbs are specified in a recipe.
- Medium eggs should be used except where otherwise specified. Free-range eggs are recommended.
- Note that certain recipes, including mayonnaise, lemon curd and some cold desserts, contain raw or lightly cooked eggs. The young, elderly, pregnant women and anyone with an immune-deficiency disease should avoid these, because of the slight risk of salmonella.
- Calorie, fat and carbohydrate counts per serving are provided for the recipes.
- If you are following a gluten- or dairy-free diet, check the labels on all pre-packaged food goods.
- Recipe serving suggestions do not take gluten- or dairy-free diets into account.

Picture credits
Photographers: Neil Barclay (pages 82, 110, 121, 126); Martin
Brigdale (pages 32, 86, 87, 91, 92, 94, 97, 101, 102, 103, 104,
107); Nicki Dowey (pages 34, 35, 37, 38, 39, 40, 41, 42, 43, 44,
45, 46, 47, 63, 51, 52, 54, 56, 61, 67, 69, 70, 71, 72, 74, 75, 77,
78, 79, 80, 81, 89, 100, 113, 114, 115, 116, 122, 123, 124); Will
Heap (pages 53, 60, 106); Craig Robertson (Basics photography
plus pages 55, 58, 59, 90, 95, 96, 99, 111, 118, 119); Lucinda
Symons (pages 28, 68)

Contents

Foreword

Pasta, rice and noodles – they're our everyday storecupboard staples. No matter how little time you have to cook supper, something wonderful and satisfying can be rustled up easily out of one of these basics. With a wide variety of each, there's always something different to cook.

Flick to the section on basics to find out the best cooking methods. Each is different but you're aiming for a similar result every time – pasta, rice and noodles should all have a slight bite when cooked. There's also step-by-step instructions for making fresh pasta from scratch – it's easy and only needs a few ingredients. Once it's cooked, toss with extra virgin olive oil, a few shavings of Parmesan and freshly ground black pepper and tuck in.

We have a tantalising choice of nutritious salads and a moreish selection of warming soups. There are simple midweek suppers such as Prawn, Courgette and Leek Risotto and Pasta with Chicken, Cream and Basil. Plus we've thrown in lots of great recipes that are ideal when you're having a more relaxed meal with friends.

Whether you're a first-timer or an accomplished cook, you'll find something in here for any occasion. All the recipes have been triple tested – so you know they'll both look and taste delicious the very first time you make them.

Emma

Emma Marsden
Cookery Editor
Good Housekeeping

The Basics

Making fresh pasta

Although you can buy good-quality fresh pasta, it's easy and fun to make at home. And while a pasta machine will make quick work of rolling and cutting, you can do it all by hand.

Fresh Pasta

To make pasta to serve three to four, you will need: 300–400g (11–14oz) flour (see Cook's Tips), 4 medium eggs, beaten, 1 tbsp extra virgin olive oil.

1 Sift 300g (11oz) flour on to a clean worksurface. Make a well in the centre, then add the eggs and oil. Draw in the flour until the mixture resembles breadcrumbs.

2 When the flour and eggs are combined, knead the dough for 5–10 minutes until smooth and elastic. Wrap in clingfilm and leave to rest for 1 hour.

3 Dust the dough and worksurface with flour and roll out until you can see the worksurface through it.

4 Hang the pasta over a rolling pin and leave to dry on the board until it no longer feels damp, then cut (see opposite).

Cook's Tips

For the best results, use Italian '00' strong flour.
When you're rolling out the pasta, have something ready to hang it on – a clothes drier or a rolling pin is perfect for this.

Herb pasta

Sift the flour and salt into the bowl and stir in 3 tbsp freshly chopped mixed herbs, such as basil, marjoram and parsley. Continue as for the basic pasta dough.

Cutting pasta with a knife

1 Lay the sheet of dough on a floured worksurface and dust lightly with flour. Lift one edge and fold it over, then keep folding to make a long, flat cigar-shape.

2 Cut the dough into strips of the required width. Unfold and leave them to dry on a clean teatowel for a few minutes before cooking.

Using a pasta machine

1 Make the pasta dough (see left) to the end of step 2. Cut the dough into small pieces that will fit through the machine's rollers. Dust the pasta with flour. Set the rollers as wide apart as they will go, then feed the dough through. Repeat two or three times, folding the dough into three after each roll.

2 Narrow the rollers and repeat. Continue until the pasta is of the right thickness, then cut as required.

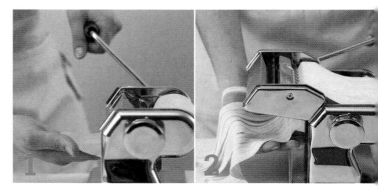

Filling ravioli

1 Lay a sheet of dough over a ravioli tray and gently press into the indentations. Place teaspoonfuls of filling into the hollows. Be particularly careful not to overfill the ravioli as the filling may leak out during cooking. Lay a second sheet of pasta on top of the first.

2 Using a wheel cutter, cut the rows vertically between the lumps of filling in one direction, then cut horizontally in the other direction to make squares. Press the edges to seal the dough.

3 Separate the ravioli, dust very lightly with flour and cover with a clean teatowel until needed. This will help prevent the ravioli from drying out while you are making more of them.

Making filled pasta shapes

1 Make the pasta dough (see left) to the end of step 2. Cut the dough into small pieces and roll out just one piece at a time. Keep the rest covered in clingfilm to prevent it from drying out.

2 Trim one edge to make a straight line, then cut a strip about 5cm (2in) from the straight edge. Cut into pieces about 5cm (2in) square.

3 Place a teaspoonful of filling at the centre of one square, then fold over to make a triangle. Do not overfill. Press the edges to seal.

4 Fold the topmost corner of the triangle down, then fold the other two edges over to leave a hollow space in the middle of the pasta. Press the two folded corners together firmly. Repeat with the remaining pasta and filling.

Cooking pasta, rice and noodles

The popular staples of pasta, noodles and rice transform meat, poultry, fish and vegetable dishes into substantial meals. Perfectly cooked rice and pasta are super-quick accompaniments, while noodles can be served alongside stir-fried dishes or added as one of the ingredients.

Cooking pasta

There are a number of mistaken ideas about cooking pasta, such as adding oil to the water, rinsing the pasta after cooking and adding salt only at a certain point. The basics couldn't be simpler. Add salt to the water before adding the pasta. Filled pasta is the only type of pasta that needs oil in the cooking water – the oil reduces friction, which could tear the wrappers and allow the filling to come out. Use 1 tbsp for a large pan of water. Rinse the pasta after cooking only if you are going to cool it for serving as salad, then drain well and toss with oil.

Dried pasta

1   Heat the water with about 1 tsp salt per 100g (3½oz) of pasta. Bring to a rolling boil, then put in all the pasta and stir well for 30 seconds, to keep the pasta from sticking.

2   Once the water is boiling again, set the timer for 2 minutes less than the cooking time on the pack and cook uncovered. Check the pasta when the timer goes off, then every 60 seconds until it is cooked al dente: tender with a little bite at the centre.

3   Drain the pasta in a colander. Toss with your chosen sauce.

Fresh pasta

Fresh pasta is cooked in the same way as dried, but for a shorter time.

1   Bring the water to the boil. Add the pasta to the boiling water all at once and stir well. Set the timer for 2 minutes and keep testing every 30 seconds until the pasta is cooked al dente: tender with a little bite at the centre.

Basic sauces

Bolognese Sauce

To serve six, you will need:
2 tbsp olive oil, 1 onion, finely chopped, 2 garlic cloves, crushed, 450g (1lb) extra-lean minced beef, 2 tbsp sun-dried tomato paste, 300ml (½ pint) red wine, 400g can chopped tomatoes, 125g (4oz) chestnut mushrooms, sliced, 2 tbsp Worcestershire sauce, salt and ground black pepper.

1 Heat the oil in a large pan, add the onion and fry over a medium heat for 10 minutes until softened and golden. Add the garlic and cook for 1 minute.

2 Add the beef and brown evenly, using a wooden spoon to break up the pieces. Stir in the tomato paste and wine, cover and bring to the boil. Add the tomatoes, mushrooms and Worcestershire sauce and season well with salt and pepper. Bring back to the boil, lower the heat and simmer for 20 minutes.

Classic Tomato Sauce

To serve four, you will need:
1 tbsp olive oil, 1 small onion, chopped, 1 carrot, grated, 1 celery stick, chopped, 1 garlic clove, crushed, ½ tbsp tomato purée, 2 x 400g cans plum tomatoes, 1 bay leaf, ½ tsp oregano, 2 tsp caster sugar, 3 tbsp freshly chopped basil, salt and ground black pepper.

1 Heat the oil in a large pan. Add the onion, carrot and celery and fry gently for 20 minutes until softened.

2 Add the garlic and tomato purée and fry for 1 minute. Stir in the tomatoes and add the bay leaf, oregano and sugar. Simmer for 30 minutes until thickened.

3 Stir the basil into the sauce and check the seasoning.

Pesto

Use on pasta or in salad dressings, mixed into crème fraîche for dips, or spread on toasted ciabatta and topped with cheese and tomato.

To serve four, you will need:
50g (2oz) fresh basil leaves, roughly torn, 1–2 garlic cloves, 25g (1oz) pinenuts, 6 tbsp extra virgin olive oil, 2 tbsp freshly grated Parmesan, lemon juice (optional), salt and ground black pepper.

1 Put the basil leaves in a food processor with the garlic, pinenuts and 2 tbsp olive oil. Blend to a fairly smooth paste. Gradually add the remaining oil and season with salt and pepper.

2 Transfer to a bowl and stir in the Parmesan. Check the seasoning and add a squeeze of lemon juice if you like. Store in the refrigerator: cover with a thin layer of olive oil and seal tightly. It will keep for up to three days.

Variations

Coriander Pesto Use fresh coriander instead of basil and add 1 seeded and finely chopped chilli with the garlic. Omit the cheese.
Rocket Pesto Replace the basil with rocket leaves and add 1 tbsp freshly chopped parsley.
Sun-dried Tomato Pesto Replace half the basil with 50g (2oz) sun-dried tomatoes, drained of oil and roughly chopped.

Cooking rice

There are two main types of rice: long-grain and short-grain. Long-grain rice is generally served as an accompaniment, while short-grain rice is used for dishes such as risotto, sushi and paella. Long-grain rice needs no special preparation, although basmati should be washed to remove excess starch.

Long-grain rice

1 Use 50–75g (2–3oz) raw rice per person; measured by volume 50–75ml (2–2½fl oz). Measure the rice by volume and put it in a pan with a pinch of salt and twice the volume of boiling water (or stock).

2 Bring to the boil. Turn the heat down to low and set the timer for the time stated on the pack. The rice should be al dente: tender with a bite at the centre.

3 When the rice is cooked, fluff up the grains with a fork.

Basmati rice

Put the rice in a bowl and cover with cold water. Stir until this becomes cloudy, then drain and repeat until the water is clear. Soak the rice for 30 minutes, then drain before cooking.

Basic Risotto

Italian risotto is made with medium-grain arborio, vialone nano or carnaroli rice, which release starch to give a rich, creamy texture. It is traditionally cooked on the hob, but can also be cooked in the oven by adding all the liquid in one go and cooking until the liquid is absorbed.

To serve four, you will need:
1 onion, chopped, 50g (2oz) butter, 900ml (1½ pints) hot chicken stock, 225g (8oz) risotto rice, 50g (2oz) freshly grated Parmesan, plus extra to serve.

1 Gently fry the onion in the butter for 10–15 minutes until very lightly coloured. Heat the stock in a separate pan and keep at a simmer. Add the rice to the butter and stir for 1–2 minutes until well coated.

2 Add a ladleful of stock and stir constantly until absorbed. Add the remaining stock a ladleful at a time, stirring, until the rice is al dente (tender but still with bite at the centre), 20–30 minutes (you may not need all the stock). Stir in the Parmesan and serve immediately with extra cheese.

Cooking noodles

Egg (wheat) noodles

These are the most versatile of Asian noodles. Like Italian pasta, they are made from wheat flour, egg and water and are available fresh or dried in various thicknesses.

1 Bring a pan of water to the boil and put the noodles in.

2 Agitate the noodles using chopsticks or a fork to separate them. This can take a minute or even more.

3 Continue boiling for 4–5 minutes until the noodles are cooked al dente: tender but with a little bite in the centre.

4 Drain well and then rinse in cold water and toss with a little oil if you are not using them immediately.

Glass, cellophane or bean thread noodles

These very thin noodles are made from mung beans; they need only 1 minute in boiling water.

Rice noodles

These may be very fine (rice vermicelli) or thick and flat. Most need no cooking, only soaking in warm or hot water; check the packet instructions, or cover the noodles with freshly boiled water and soak until they are al dente: tender but with a little bite at the centre. Drain well and toss with a little oil if you are not using them immediately.

Perfect noodles

Use 50–75g (2–3oz) uncooked noodles per person.
Dried egg noodles are often packed in layers. As a general rule, allow one layer per person for a main dish.
If you plan to re-cook the noodles after the initial boiling or soaking – for example, in a stir-fry – it's best to undercook them slightly.
When cooking a layer, block or nest of noodles, use a pair of forks or chopsticks to untangle the strands from the moment they go into the water.

Preparing vegetables

Just a few basic techniques will help you to prepare all these frequently used vegetables ready for quick cooking in your pasta, noodle and rice dishes.

Onions

1 Cut off the tip and base of the onion. Peel away all the layers of papery skin and any discoloured layers underneath.

2 Put the onion root end down on the chopping board, then, using a sharp knife, cut the onion in half from tip to base.

3 **Slicing** Put one half on the board with the cut surface facing down and slice across the onion.

4 **Chopping** Slice the halved onions from the root end to the top at regular intervals. Next, make 2–3 horizontal slices through the onion, then slice vertically across the width.

Shallots

1 Cut off the tip and trim off the ends of the root. Peel off the skin and any discoloured layers underneath.

2 Holding the shallot with the root end down, use a small sharp knife to make deep parallel slices almost down to the base while keeping the slices attached to it.

3 **Slicing** Turn the shallot on its side and cut off slices from the base.

4 **Dicing** Make deep parallel slices at right angles to the first slices. Turn the shallot on its side and cut off the slices from the base. You should now have fine dice, but chop any larger pieces individually.

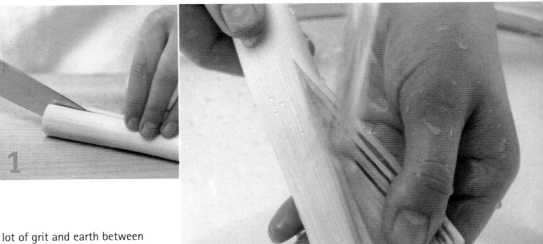

Leeks

As some leeks harbour a lot of grit and earth between their leaves, they need careful cleaning.

1 Cut off the root and any tough parts. Make a cut into the leaf end of the leek, about 7.5cm (3in) deep.

2 Hold under the cold tap while separating the cut halves to expose any grit. Wash well, then shake dry. Slice or cut into matchsticks.

Mushrooms

Button, white, chestnut and flat mushrooms are all prepared in a similar way.

1 Wipe with a damp cloth or pastry brush to remove any dirt.

2 Button mushrooms: cut off the stalk flush with the cap base. Other mushrooms: cut a thin disc off the end of the stalk and discard. Chop or slice the mushrooms.

Asparagus

1 Cut or snap off the woody stem of each asparagus spear about 5cm (2in) from the stalk end, or where the white and green sections meet. Or cut off the stalk end and peel with a vegetable peeler or small sharp knife.

Cabbage

The crinkly-leaved Savoy cabbage may need more washing than other varieties, because its open leaves catch dirt more easily than the tightly packed white and red cabbage. The following method is suitable for all cabbages, including mild-flavoured Chinese leaves or Chinese cabbage.

1 Pick off any of the outer leaves that are dry, tough or discoloured. Cut off the base and, using a small sharp knife, cut out as much as possible of the tough inner core in a single cone-shaped piece.

2 If you need whole cabbage leaves, peel them off one by one. As you work your way down, you will need to cut out more of the core.

3 If you are cooking the cabbage in wedges, cut it in half lengthways, then cut the pieces into wedges of the required size.

Shredding cabbage

Cut the cabbage into quarters, then slice with a large cook's knife. Alternatively, use the shredding disc of a food processor.

Pak choi

Also known as bok choy, pak choi is a type of cabbage that does not form a heart. It has dark green leaves and thick fleshy white stalks, which are sometimes cooked separately.

Broccoli

1 Slice off the end of the stalk and cut 1cm (½in) below the florets. Cut the broccoli head in half.

2 Peel the thick, woody skin from the stalks and slice the stalks in half or quarters lengthways. Cut off equal-sized florets with a small knife. If the florets are very large, or if you want them for a stir-fry, you can halve them by cutting lengthways through the stalk and pulling the two halves apart.

Carrots

1 **Paring ribbons** Cut off the ends, then, using a vegetable peeler, peel off the skin and discard. Continue peeling the carrot into ribbon strips.

2 **Slicing** Cut slices off each of the rounded sides to make four flat surfaces that are stable on the chopping board. Hold steady with one hand and cut lengthways into even slices so they are lying in a flat stack. The stack can then be cut into batons or matchsticks.

Cutting tomatoes

1 Use a small sharp knife to cut out the core in a single cone-shaped piece. Discard the core.

2 **Wedges** Halve the tomato and then cut into quarters or into three.

3 **Slices** Hold the tomato with the cored side on the chopping board for greater stability and use a serrated knife to cut into slices.

Seeding tomatoes

1 Halve the tomato through the core. Use a spoon or a small sharp knife to remove the seeds and juice. Shake off the excess liquid.

2 Chop the tomato as required for your recipe and place in a colander for a minute or two, to drain off any excess liquid.

Peeling tomatoes

1 Fill a bowl or pan with boiling water. Using a slotted spoon, carefully add the tomato and leave for 15–30 seconds, then remove to a chopping board.

2 Use a small sharp knife to cut out the core in a single cone-shaped piece. Discard the core.

3 Peel off the skin; it should come away easily, depending on ripeness.

Perfect vegetables

Wash vegetables before you cut them up, to retain as many nutrients as possible.
Cook as soon as possible after you have cut them.
Do not overcook vegetables or they will lose their bright colour, crisp texture and some of their nutrients.

Avocados

Prepare avocados just before serving because their flesh discolours quickly once exposed to air.

1 Halve the avocado lengthways and twist the two halves apart. Tap the stone with a sharp knife, then twist to remove the stone.

2 Run a knife between the flesh and skin and pull away. Slice the flesh.

Courgettes

Cutting diagonally is ideal for courgettes and other vegetables in a stir-fry.

Seeding peppers

The seeds and white pith of peppers taste bitter so should be removed.

1 Cut off the top of the pepper, then cut away and discard the seeds and white pith.

2 Alternatively, cut the pepper in half vertically and snap out the white pithy core and seeds. Trim away the rest of the white membrane with a knife.

Chargrilling peppers

Charring imparts a smoky flavour and makes peppers easier to peel.

1 Hold the pepper, using tongs, over the gas flame on your hob (or put under a preheated grill) until the skin blackens, turning until black all over.

2 Put in a bowl, cover and leave to cool (the steam will help to loosen the skin). Peel.

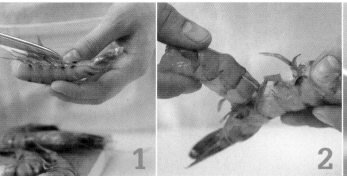

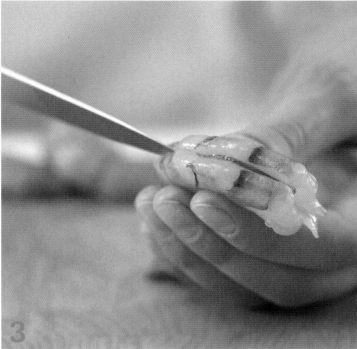

Preparing shellfish

Always buy shellfish from a reputable fishmonger or a supermarket fresh fish counter with a high turnover, and then prepare them within 24 hours. Most shellfish from supermarkets has been previously frozen, so don't re-freeze it.

Prawns

Prawns are delicious stir-fried. They can be completely shelled, or you can leave the tail on, but they should be deveined before using.

1   Pull off the head and discard (or put to one side and use later for making stock). Using pointed scissors, cut through the soft shell on the belly side.

2   Prise the shell off, leaving the tail attached. (The shell can also be used later for making stock.)

3   Using a small sharp knife, make a shallow cut along the back of the prawn. Using the point of the knife, remove and discard the black vein (the intestinal tract) that runs along the back of the prawn.

Mussels

Mussels take moments to cook, but careful preparation is important, so give yourself enough time to get the shellfish ready.

1   Scrape off the fibres attached to the shells (beards). If the mussels are very clean, give them a quick rinse under the cold tap. If they are very sandy, scrub them with a stiff brush, then rinse thoroughly.

2   If the shells have sizeable barnacles on them, it's best (though not essential) to remove them. Rap them sharply with a metal spoon or the back of a washing-up brush, then scrape off.

3   Discard any open mussels that don't shut when sharply tapped; this means they are dead and may cause food poisoning.

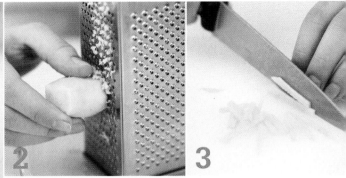

Flavourings

Many stir-fry recipes begin by cooking garlic, ginger and spring onions as the basic flavourings. Spicier dishes may include chillies, lemongrass or a prepared spice paste such as Thai curry paste.

Ginger

1 **Grating** Cut off a piece of the root and peel with a vegetable peeler. Cut off any brown spots.

2 Rest the grater on a board or small plate and grate the ginger. Discard any large fibres adhering to the pulp.

3 **Slicing, shredding and chopping** Cut slices off the ginger and cut off the skin carefully. Cut off any brown spots. Stack the slices and cut into shreds. To chop, stack the shreds and cut across into small pieces.

4 **Pressing** If you just need the ginger juice, peel and cut off any brown spots, then cut into small chunks and use a garlic press held over a small bowl to extract the juice.

Lemongrass

Lemongrass is a popular South-east Asian ingredient, giving an aromatic lemony flavour. It looks rather like a long, slender spring onion, but is fibrous and woody and is usually removed before the dish is served. Alternatively, the inner leaves may be very finely chopped or pounded in a mortar and pestle and used in spice pastes.

Spring onions

Cut off the roots and trim any coarse or withered green parts. Slice diagonally, or shred by cutting into 5cm (2in) lengths, then slicing down the lengths, or chop finely, according to the recipe.

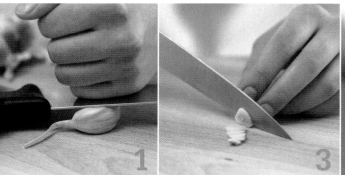

Garlic

1 Put the clove on a chopping board and place the flat side of a large knife on top of it. Press down firmly on the flat of the blade to crush the clove and break the papery skin.

2 Cut off the base of the clove and slip the garlic out of its skin. It should come away easily.

3 **Slicing** Using a rocking motion with the knife tip on the board, slice the garlic as thinly as you need.

4 **Shredding and chopping** Holding the slices together, shred them across the slices. Chop the shreds if you need chopped garlic.

5 **Crushing** After step 2, the whole clove can be put into a garlic press. To crush with a knife: roughly chop the peeled cloves with a pinch of salt. Press down hard with the edge of a large knife tip (with the blade facing away from you), then drag the blade along the garlic while still pressing hard. Continue to do this, dragging the knife tip over the garlic.

Chillies

1 Cut off the cap and slit open lengthways. Using a spoon, scrape out the seeds and the pith.

2 For diced chilli, cut into thin shreds lengthways, then cut crossways.

Cook's Tip

Wash hands thoroughly after handling chillies – the volatile oils will sting if accidentally rubbed into your eyes.

The Asian storecupboard

Rice and noodles are the staple foods; see pages 14–15. The following items, used in many Asian dishes, are available in most large supermarkets and Asian food shops.

Spices

Chinese five-spice powder is made from star anise, fennel seeds, cinnamon, cloves and Sichuan pepper. It has a strong liquorice-like flavour and should be used sparingly.

Kaffir lime leaves, used in South-east Asian cooking for their lime-lemon flavour, are glossy leaves used whole but not eaten – rather like bay leaves. Use grated lime zest as a substitute.

Tamarind paste has a delicately sour flavour; use lemon juice as a substitute.

Sauces

Black bean sauce is made from fermented black beans, salt and ginger. Salty and pungent on its own, it adds richness to many stir-fry dishes.

Chilli sauce is made from fresh red chillies, vinegar, salt and sugar; some versions include other ingredients such as garlic or ginger. Sweet chilli sauce is a useful standby for adding piquancy to all kinds of dishes.

Hoisin sauce, sometimes called barbecue sauce, is a thick, sweet-spicy red-brown sauce.

Oyster sauce is a smooth brown sauce made from oyster extract, wheat flour and other flavourings. It doesn't taste fishy, but adds a 'meaty' flavour to stir-fries and braises.

Plum sauce, made from plums, ginger, chillies, vinegar and sugar, is traditionally served with duck or as a dip.

Soy sauce – made from fermented soya beans and, usually, wheat – is the most common flavouring in Chinese and South-east Asian cooking. There are light and dark soy sauces; the dark kind is slightly sweeter and tends to darken the food. It will keep indefinitely.

Thai fish sauce is a salty condiment with a distinctive, pungent aroma. It is used in many South-east Asian dishes. You can buy it in most large supermarkets and Asian food stores. It will keep indefinitely.

Thai green curry paste is a blend of spices such as green chillies, coriander and lemongrass.

Thai red curry paste contains fresh and dried red chillies and ginger. Once opened, store in a sealed container in the refrigerator for up to one month.

Yellow bean sauce is a thick, salty, aromatic yellow-brown purée of fermented yellow soy beans, flour and salt.

Canned vegetables

Bamboo shoots, available sliced or in chunks, have a mild flavour; rinse before use.

Water chestnuts have a very mild flavour but add a lovely crunch to stir-fried and braised dishes.

Other ingredients

Canned coconut milk is widely available, but if you can't find it, use blocks of creamed coconut or coconut powder, following the packet instructions to make the amount of liquid you need.

Dried mushrooms feature in some Chinese recipes; they need to be soaked in hot water for 30 minutes before use.

Dried shrimps and dried shrimp paste (blachan) are often used in South-east Asian cooking. The pungent smell becomes milder during cooking and marries with the other ingredients. These are often included in ready-made sauces and spice pastes, and are not suitable for vegetarians.

Mirin is a sweet rice wine from Japan; if you can't find it, use dry or medium sherry instead.

Rice vinegar is clear and milder than other vinegars. Use white wine vinegar or cider vinegar as a substitute.

Rice wine is often used in Chinese cooking; if you can't find it, use dry sherry instead.

Which oil to use?

Groundnut (peanut) oil has a mild flavour and is widely used in China and South-east Asia. It is well suited to stir-frying and deep-frying as it has a high smoke point and can therefore be used at high temperatures.
It usually has a bland flavour and is suitable for stir-frying.

Sesame oil has a distinctive nutty flavour; it is best used in marinades or added as a seasoning to stir-fried dishes just before serving.

Vegetable oil may be pure rapeseed oil, or a blend of corn, soya bean, rapeseed or other oils.

Washing

1 Trim the roots and part of the stalks from the herbs. Immerse in cold water and shake briskly. Leave in the water for a few minutes.

2 Lift out of the water and put in a colander or sieve, then rinse again under the cold tap. Leave to drain for a few minutes, then dry thoroughly on kitchen paper or teatowels, or use a salad spinner.

Chopping

1 Trim the herbs by pinching off all but the smallest, most tender stalks. If the herb is one with a woody stalk, such as rosemary or thyme, it may be easier to remove the leaves by rubbing the whole bunch between your hands; the leaves should simply pull off the stems.

2 If you are chopping the leaves, gather them into a compact ball in one hand, keeping your fist around the ball (but being careful not to crush them).

3 Chop with a large knife, using a rocking motion and letting just a little of the ball out of your fingers at a time.

4 When the herbs are roughly chopped, continue chopping until the pieces are in small shreds or flakes.

Using herbs

Most herbs are the leaf of a flowering plant and are usually sold with much of the stalk intact. They have to be washed, trimmed and then chopped or torn into pieces suitable for your recipe.

Perfect herbs

- Don't pour the herbs and their water into the sieve, because dirt in the water might get caught in the leaves.
- If the herb has fleshy stalks, such as parsley or coriander, the stalks can be saved to flavour stock or soup. Tie them in a bundle with string for easy removal.

Making stock

Good stock can make the difference between a good dish and a great one. It gives depth of flavour to many dishes.

Cook's Tips

To get a clearer liquid when making fish, meat or poultry stock, strain the cooked stock through four layers of muslin in a sieve.

Stock will keep for three days in the refrigerator. If you want to keep it for a further three days, transfer it to a pan and reboil gently for five minutes. Cool, put in a clean bowl and chill for a further three days.

When making meat or chicken stock, make sure there is a good ratio of meat to bones. The more meat you use, the more flavour the stock will have.

Stocks

Vegetable Stock

For 1.1 litres (2 pints), you will need:
225g (8oz) each onions, celery, leeks and carrots, chopped, 2 bay leaves, a few thyme sprigs, 1 small bunch parsley, 10 black peppercorns, ½ tsp salt.

1 Put all the ingredients in a pan and pour in 1.7 litres (3 pints) cold water.

2 Bring slowly to the boil and skim the surface. Partially cover and simmer for 30 minutes. Adjust the seasoning. Strain the stock through a fine sieve into a bowl and leave to cool.

Meat Stock

For 900ml (1½ pints), you will need:
450g (1lb) each meat bones and stewing meat, 1 onion, 2 celery sticks and 1 large carrot, sliced, 1 bouquet garni (2 bay leaves, a few thyme sprigs and a small bunch parsley), 1 tsp black peppercorns, ½ tsp salt.

1 Preheat the oven to 220°C (200°C fan oven) mark 7. Put the meat and bones in a roasting tin and roast for 30–40 minutes, turning now and again, until they are well browned.

2 Put the bones and meat in a large pan with the remaining ingredients and add 2 litres (3½ pints) cold water. Bring slowly to the boil and skim the surface. Partially cover and simmer for 4–5 hours. Adjust the seasoning. Strain through a muslin-lined sieve into a bowl and cool quickly. Degrease (see opposite) before using.

Chicken Stock

For 1.1 litres (2 pints), you will need:
1.6kg (3½lb) chicken bones, 225g (8oz) each onions
and celery, sliced, 150g (5oz) chopped leeks,
1 bouquet garni (2 bay leaves, a few thyme sprigs
and a small bunch parsley), 1 tsp black peppercorns,
½ tsp salt.

1 Put all the ingredients in a large pan with
3 litres (5¼ pints) cold water.

2 Bring slowly to the boil and skim the surface.
Partially cover the pan and simmer gently for
2 hours. Adjust the seasoning if necessary.

3 Strain the stock through a muslin-lined
sieve into a bowl (see Cook's Tips) and cool
quickly. Degrease (see right) before using.

Fish Stock

For 900ml (1½ pints), you will need:
900g (2lb) fish bones and trimmings, washed,
2 carrots, 1 onion and 2 celery sticks, sliced,
1 bouquet garni (2 bay leaves, a few thyme sprigs
and a small bunch parsley), 6 white peppercorns,
½ tsp salt.

1 Put all the ingredients in a large pan with
900ml (1½ pints) cold water.

2 Bring slowly to the boil and skim the surface.
Partially cover the pan and simmer gently for
30 minutes. Adjust the seasoning if necessary.

3 Strain through a muslin-lined sieve into a bowl
and cool quickly. Fish stock tends not to have
much fat in it and so does not usually need to
be degreased. However, if it does seem to be
fatty, you will need to remove the fat by
degreasing (see right).

Degreasing stock

Meat and poultry stock needs to be degreased. (Vegetable
stock does not.) You can mop the fat from the surface
using kitchen paper, but the following methods are easier
and more effective. There are three main methods that you
can use: ladling, pouring and chilling.

1 **Ladling** While the stock is warm, place a ladle on
the surface. Press down to allow the fat floating on
the surface to trickle over the edge until the ladle is
full. Discard the fat, then repeat until all the fat has
been removed.

2 **Pouring** For this you need a degreasing jug or a
double-pouring gravy boat, which has the spout
at the base of the vessel. When you fill the jug or
gravy boat with a fatty liquid, the fat rises. When you
pour, the stock comes out while the fat stays behind
in the jug.

3 **Chilling** This technique works best with stock made
from meat, whose fat solidifies when cold. Put the
stock in the refrigerator until the fat becomes solid,
then remove the pieces of fat using a slotted spoon.

Food storage and hygiene

Storing food properly and preparing it in a hygienic way is important to ensure that food remains as nutritious and flavourful as possible, and to reduce the risk of food poisoning.

Hygiene

When you are preparing food, always follow these important guidelines:

Wash your hands thoroughly before handling food and again between handling different types of food, such as raw and cooked meat and poultry. If you have any cuts or grazes on your hands, be sure to keep them covered with a waterproof plaster.

Wash down worksurfaces regularly with a mild detergent solution or multi-surface cleaner.

Use a dishwasher if available. Otherwise, wear rubber gloves for washing-up, so that the water temperature can be hotter than unprotected hands can bear. Change drying-up cloths and cleaning cloths regularly. Note that leaving dishes to drain is more hygienic than drying them with a teatowel.

Keep raw and cooked foods separate, especially meat, fish and poultry. Wash kitchen utensils in between preparing raw and cooked foods. Never put cooked or ready-to-eat foods directly on to a surface that has just had raw fish, meat or poultry on it.

Keep pets out of the kitchen if possible; or make sure they stay away from worksurfaces. Never allow animals on to worksurfaces.

Shopping

Always choose fresh ingredients in prime condition from stores and markets that have a regular turnover of stock to ensure you buy the freshest produce possible.

Make sure items are within their 'best before' or 'use by' date. (Foods with a longer shelf life have a 'best before' date; more perishable items have a 'use by' date.)

Pack frozen and chilled items in an insulated cool bag at the check-out and put them into the freezer or refrigerator as soon as you get home.

During warm weather in particular, buy perishable foods just before you return home. When packing items at the check-out, sort them according to where you will store them when you get home – the refrigerator, freezer, storecupboard, vegetable rack, fruit bowl, etc. This will make unpacking easier – and quicker.

The storecupboard

Although storecupboard ingredients will generally last a long time, correct storage is important:

Always check packaging for storage advice – even with familiar foods, because storage requirements may change if additives, sugar or salt have been reduced. Check storecupboard foods for their 'best before' or 'use by' date and do not use them if the date has passed.

Keep all food cupboards scrupulously clean and make sure food containers and packets are properly sealed.

Once opened, treat canned foods as though fresh. Always transfer the contents to a clean container, cover and keep in the refrigerator. Similarly, jars, sauce bottles and cartons should be kept chilled after opening. (Check the label for safe storage times after opening.)

Transfer dry goods such as sugar, rice and pasta to moisture-proof containers. When supplies are used up, wash the container well and thoroughly dry before refilling with new supplies.

Store oils in a dark cupboard away from any heat source as heat and light can make them turn rancid and affect their colour. For the same reason, buy olive oil in dark green bottles.

Store vinegars in a cool place; they can turn bad in a warm environment.

Store dried herbs, spices and flavourings in a cool, dark cupboard or in dark jars. Buy in small quantities as their flavour will not last indefinitely.

Store flours and sugars in airtight containers.

Refrigerator storage

Fresh food needs to be kept in the cool temperature of the refrigerator to keep it in good condition and discourage the growth of harmful bacteria. Store day-to-day perishable items, such as opened jams and jellies, mayonnaise and bottled sauces, in the refrigerator along with eggs and dairy products, fruit juices, bacon, fresh and cooked meat (on separate shelves), and salads and vegetables (except potatoes, which don't suit being stored in the cold). A refrigerator should be kept at an operating temperature of 4–5°C.

It is worth investing in a refrigerator thermometer to ensure the correct temperature is maintained. To ensure your refrigerator is functioning effectively for safe food storage, follow these guidelines:

To avoid bacterial cross-contamination, store cooked and raw foods on separate shelves, putting cooked foods on the top shelf. Ensure that all items are well wrapped.

Never put hot food into the refrigerator, as this will cause the internal temperature of the refrigerator to rise.

Avoid overfilling the refrigerator, as this restricts the circulation of air and prevents the appliance from working properly.

It can take some time for the refrigerator to return to the correct operating temperature once the door has been opened, so don't leave it open any longer than is necessary.

Clean the refrigerator regularly, using a specially formulated germicidal refrigerator cleaner. Alternatively, use a weak solution of bicarbonate of soda: 1 tbsp to 1 litre (1³/4 pints) water.

If your refrigerator doesn't have an automatic defrost facility, defrost regularly.

Maximum refrigerator storage times

For pre-packed foods, always adhere to the 'use by' date on the packet. For other foods the following storage times should apply, providing the food is in prime condition when it goes into the refrigerator and that your refrigerator is in good working order.

Vegetables and Fruit

Green vegetables	3–4 days
Salad leaves	2–3 days
Hard and stone fruit	3–7 days
Soft fruit	1–2 days

Dairy Food

Cheese, hard	1 week
Cheese, soft	2–3 days
Eggs	1 week
Milk	4–5 days

Fish

Fish	1 day
Shellfish	1 day

Raw Meat

Bacon	7 days
Game	2 days
Joints	3 days
Minced meat	1 day
Offal	1 day
Poultry	2 days
Raw sliced meat	2 days
Sausages	3 days

Cooked Meat

Joints	3 days
Casseroles/stews	2 days
Sliced meat	2 days
Ham	2 days
Ham, vacuum-packed (or according to the instructions on the packet)	1–2 weeks

Soups and Salads

Cook's Tip

Dried galangal, similar in flavour to root ginger, needs to be soaked for 30 minutes before using. It's used chopped or grated in many Thai, Indonesian and Malaysian dishes.

Thai Chicken and Noodle Soup

225g (8oz) firm tofu

vegetable oil for shallow-frying or deep-frying

2.5cm (1in) piece fresh root ginger, peeled and finely chopped

2.5cm (1in) piece fresh or dried galangal, peeled and thinly sliced (optional, see Cook's Tip)

1–2 garlic cloves, crushed

2 lemongrass stalks, halved lengthways and bruised

1 tsp chilli powder

½ tsp ground turmeric

275g (10oz) cooked chicken, skinned and cut into bite-sized pieces

175g (6oz) cauliflower, broken into small florets and any thick stems sliced thinly

1 large carrot, peeled and cut into matchsticks

600ml (1 pint) coconut milk

600ml (1 pint) chicken or vegetable stock, or water

a few green beans, halved

125g (4oz) fine or medium egg noodles

125g (4oz) cooked and peeled prawns (optional)

3 spring onions, thinly sliced

75g (3oz) bean sprouts

2 tbsp soy sauce

1 Pat the tofu dry with kitchen paper, then cut it into small cubes, about 1cm (½in) square. Heat the oil in a deep-fryer to 180°C (test by frying a small cube of bread; it should brown in 40 seconds). Fry the tofu, in batches, until golden brown on all sides, about 1 minute. Drain on kitchen paper. Alternatively, shallow-fry the tofu in a wok.

2 Heat 2 tbsp oil in a large pan. Add the ginger, galangal, if using, garlic, lemongrass, chilli powder, turmeric and chicken and cook for 2 minutes, stirring all the time.

3 Add the cauliflower, carrot, coconut milk and stock and bring to the boil, stirring all the time. Reduce the heat and simmer for 10 minutes. Add the beans and simmer for 5 minutes.

4 Meanwhile, bring a large pan of water to the boil and cook the noodles for about 4 minutes or according to the packet instructions.

5 Drain the noodles and add them to the soup with the prawns, if using, the tofu, spring onions, bean sprouts and soy sauce. Simmer gently for 5 minutes or until heated through. Serve immediately.

A LITTLE EFFORT		NUTRITIONAL INFORMATION		Serves
Preparation Time 20 minutes	**Cooking Time** about 30 minutes	**Per Serving** 384 calories, 15g fat (of which 3g saturates), 36g carbohydrate, 2g salt	Dairy free	**4**

Hot and Sour Soup

1 tbsp vegetable oil

2 turkey breasts, about 300g (11oz), or the same quantity of tofu, cut into strips

5cm (2in) piece fresh root ginger, peeled and grated

4 spring onions, finely sliced

1–2 tbsp Thai red curry paste

75g (3oz) long-grain wild rice

1.1 litres (2 pints) hot weak chicken or vegetable stock, or boiling water

200g (7oz) mangetouts, sliced

juice of 1 lime

4 tbsp roughly chopped coriander to garnish

1 Heat the oil in a deep pan. Add the turkey or tofu and cook over a medium heat for 5 minutes or until browned. Add the ginger and spring onions and cook for a further 2–3 minutes. Stir in the curry paste and cook for 1–2 minutes to warm the spices.

2 Add the rice and stir to coat in the curry paste. Pour the hot stock or boiling water into the pan. Stir once, then bring to the boil. Lower the heat and leave to simmer, covered, for 20 minutes.

3 Add the mangetouts and cook for a further 5 minutes or until the rice is cooked. Just before serving, squeeze in the lime juice and stir to mix. Ladle into bowls and sprinkle with the coriander.

	EASY		NUTRITIONAL INFORMATION	
Serves **4**	**Preparation Time** 20 minutes	**Cooking Time** 30–35 minutes	**Per Serving** 255 calories, 10g fat (of which 1g saturates), 19g carbohydrate, 0.7g salt	Gluten free Dairy free

Cook's Tip

You can buy good-quality pesto from the supermarket, but it's easy to make yourself from fresh basil leaves, garlic, pinenuts, olive oil and Parmesan. See page 13.

Spinach and Rice Soup

4 tbsp extra virgin olive oil

1 onion, finely chopped

2 garlic cloves, crushed

2 tsp freshly chopped thyme or a large pinch of dried thyme

2 tsp freshly chopped rosemary or a large pinch of dried rosemary

grated zest of ½ lemon

2 tsp ground coriander

¼ tsp cayenne pepper

125g (4oz) arborio (risotto) rice

1.1 litres (2 pints) vegetable stock

225g (8oz) fresh or frozen and thawed spinach, shredded

4 tbsp pesto sauce (see Cook's Tip)

salt and ground black pepper

extra virgin olive oil and freshly shaved Parmesan to serve

1 Heat half the oil in a pan. Add the onion, garlic, herbs, lemon zest and spices, then fry gently for 5 minutes.

2 Add the remaining oil with the rice and cook, stirring, for 1 minute. Add the stock, bring to the boil and simmer gently for 20 minutes or until the rice is tender.

3 Stir the spinach into the soup with the pesto sauce. Cook for 2 minutes, then season to taste with salt and pepper.

4 Serve drizzled with a little oil and topped with Parmesan.

EASY		NUTRITIONAL INFORMATION		Serves
Preparation Time 10 minutes	**Cooking Time** 25–30 minutes	**Per Serving** 335 calories, 20g fat (of which 4g saturates), 29g carbohydrate, 0.7g salt	Vegetarian Gluten free	**6**

Quick Winter Minestrone

2 tbsp olive oil
1 small onion, finely chopped
1 carrot, chopped
1 celery stick, chopped
1 garlic clove, crushed
2 tbsp chopped fresh thyme
1 litre (1³/₄ pints) vegetable stock
400g can chopped tomatoes
400g can borlotti beans, drained
125g (4oz) minestrone pasta
175g (6oz) Savoy cabbage, shredded
salt and ground black pepper
fresh pesto, toasted ciabatta and extra virgin
olive oil to serve

1 Heat the oil in a large pan and add the onion, carrot and celery. Cook for 8–10 minutes until softened, then add the garlic and thyme and fry for another 2–3 minutes.

2 Add the stock, tomatoes and half the borlotti beans. Mash the remaining beans, stir into the soup and simmer for 30 minutes, adding the minestrone pasta and cabbage for the last 10 minutes of cooking time.

3 Check the seasoning, then serve the soup in individual bowls with a dollop of fresh pesto on top and slices of toasted ciabatta drizzled with extra virgin olive oil on the side.

Serves 4	EASY		NUTRITIONAL INFORMATION	
	Preparation Time 10 minutes	**Cooking Time** 45 minutes	**Per Serving** 334 calories, 11g fat (of which 2.5g saturates), 47g carbohydrate, 1.5g salt	Vegetarian

Pasta and Avocado Salad

2 tbsp mayonnaise

2 tbsp pesto

2 ripe avocados, halved, stoned, peeled and cut into cubes

225g (8oz) cooked pasta, cooled

a few basil leaves

1 Mix together the mayonnaise, pesto and avocados, then mix with the pasta. (If the dressing is too thick, dilute with a little water – use the pasta cooking water if you have it.) Decorate with basil leaves and serve as a light lunch.

	EASY		NUTRITIONAL INFORMATION	
Serves 4	**Preparation Time** 5 minutes	**Cooking Time** 15–20 minutes	**Per Serving** 313 calories, 26g fat (of which 5g saturates), 14g carbohydrate, 0.6g salt	Vegetarian

Asparagus, Pea and Mint Rice Salad

175g (6oz) mixed basmati and wild rice

1 large shallot, finely sliced

grated zest and juice of 1 small lemon

2 tbsp sunflower oil

12 fresh mint leaves, roughly chopped, plus extra sprigs to garnish

150g (5oz) asparagus tips

75g (3oz) fresh or frozen peas

salt and ground black pepper

1 Put the rice in a pan with twice its volume of water and a pinch of salt. Cover and bring to the boil. Reduce the heat to very low and cook according to the packet instructions. Once cooked, tip the rice on to a baking sheet and spread out to cool quickly. When cool, spoon into a large bowl.

2 In a small bowl, mix the shallot with the lemon zest and juice, oil and chopped mint, then stir into the rice.

3 Bring a large pan of lightly salted water to the boil. Add the asparagus and peas and cook for 3–4 minutes until tender. Drain and refresh in a bowl of cold water. Drain well and stir into the rice; season with salt and pepper. Put into a serving dish and garnish with mint sprigs.

EASY		NUTRITIONAL INFORMATION		Serves
Preparation Time 10 minutes	**Cooking Time** 20 minutes, plus cooling	**Per Serving** 157 calories, 4g fat (of which trace saturates), 26g carbohydrate, trace salt	Vegetarian Gluten free • Dairy free	**6**

Cook's Tips

Chillies vary enormously in strength, from quite mild to blisteringly hot, depending on the type of chilli and its ripeness. Taste a small piece first to check that it's not too hot for you. To prepare, see page 23.

When handling chillies, be extremely careful not to touch or rub your eyes with your fingers, as it will make them sting. Wash knives immediately after handling chillies. As a precaution, use rubber gloves when preparing them if you like.

450g (1lb) straight-to-wok medium egg noodles

2 red chillies, seeded and finely chopped (see Cook's Tips)

4 spring onions, finely sliced

½ cucumber, halved lengthways, seeded and finely diced

350g (12oz) cooked and peeled prawns

1 tbsp freshly chopped coriander

For the soy and sesame dressing

2 tbsp runny honey

2 tbsp dark soy sauce

2 tbsp rice wine vinegar

4 tbsp sesame oil

ground black pepper

Chinese Prawn Noodle Salad

1 Put the noodles into a bowl and pour in boiling water to cover them. Cover with clingfilm and leave for 5 minutes.

2 To make the dressing, whisk the honey, soy sauce, vinegar and sesame oil together with some black pepper. Drain the noodles and, while still warm, pour the dressing over them. Toss together, then leave to cool.

3 To serve, stir the chillies, spring onions, cucumber, prawns and coriander into the noodles and pile into four bowls. If you have time, chill for 30 minutes–1 hour.

Serves 4	EASY		NUTRITIONAL INFORMATION	
	Preparation Time 15 minutes, plus chilling and 5 minutes soaking		**Per Serving** 632 calories, 21g fat (of which 4g saturates), 88g carbohydrate, 2.2g salt	Dairy free

Cook's Tips

To serve this dish hot, put 5 tbsp basil-infused oil in a frying pan, add the garlic and chillies and cook for 1 minute. Add the drained pasta and mix well, then add the tomatoes and mozzarella. Garnish and serve.
Instead of mozzarella, use Gorgonzola or Brie.
You can use 1/2 tsp dried crushed chillies instead of fresh.

Tomato and Mozzarella Pasta Salad

2 tsp lemon juice

7 tbsp basil-infused olive oil

2 garlic cloves, crushed

350g (12oz) penne pasta

250g (9oz) mozzarella, cut into chunks

700g (1½lb) vine-ripened tomatoes, skinned, seeded and cut into chunks

½ large red chilli, seeded and finely sliced (see opposite)

½ large green chilli, seeded and finely sliced (see opposite)

salt and ground black pepper

fresh flat-leafed parsley or basil to garnish

1 Put some salt and pepper in a small bowl, whisk in the lemon juice, followed by the flavoured oil and garlic, then set aside.

2 Bring a large pan of salted water to the boil, add the pasta and cook according to the packet instructions. Drain well, then tip into a large bowl and toss with 2 tbsp of the dressing (this will prevent the pasta from sticking together); set aside to cool. Put the mozzarella in a large bowl with the remaining dressing and set aside.

3 When ready to serve (see Cook's Tips), add the pasta to the mozzarella with the tomatoes and chillies. Toss together and season well with salt and pepper. Garnish with parsley or basil, then serve.

EASY		NUTRITIONAL INFORMATION		Serves
Preparation Time 20 minutes, plus cooling	**Cooking Time** 10–12 minutes	**Per Serving** 665 calories, 34g fat (of which 12g saturates), 70g carbohydrate, 0.7g salt	Vegetarian	**4**

Pasta, Salami and Tapenade Salad

3 x 225g tubs pasta salad in tomato sauce

75g (3oz) pepper salami, shredded

3 tbsp black olive tapenade paste

3 tbsp freshly chopped chives

salt and ground black pepper

1 Turn the pasta salad into a large bowl, and add the salami, tapenade and chives. Toss everything together and season with pepper. Check for seasoning before adding salt – the tapenade may have made the salad salty enough.

2 Pile the salad into a large serving bowl. If not being served straight away, this salad is best kept in a cool place (but not chilled) until needed.

Serves 4	EASY	NUTRITIONAL INFORMATION	
	Preparation Time 5 minutes	**Per Serving** 332 calories, 20g fat (of which 6g saturates), 28g carbohydrate, 2g salt	Dairy free

Try Something Different

Replace the mixed seafood with 350g (12oz) cooked and peeled prawns or 300g (11oz) smoked chicken, sliced.

Warm Seafood and Pasta Salad

175g (6oz) pasta shapes
3 tbsp olive oil
1 tbsp rice wine vinegar
grated zest and juice of 2 limes
2 red chillies, seeded and finely chopped (see page 40)
250g pack cooked mixed seafood
225g (8oz) yellow cherry tomatoes, halved
1 large avocado, halved, stoned, peeled and thickly sliced
1 red onion, finely sliced
50g (2oz) green olives
3 tbsp freshly chopped coriander
salt and ground black pepper

1 Bring a large pan of water to the boil, add the pasta and cook according to the packet instructions. Drain well, then transfer to a serving dish.

2 To make the dressing, whisk the oil and vinegar together in a small bowl. Whisk the lime zest and juice and the chillies into the dressing and season to taste with salt and pepper.

3 Stir the dressing into the pasta with the seafood, tomatoes, avocado, onion, olives and coriander. Stir well and serve immediately.

EASY		NUTRITIONAL INFORMATION		Serves
Preparation Time 15 minutes	**Cooking Time** 10–12 minutes	**Per Serving** 301 calories, 10g fat (of which 2g saturates), 36g carbohydrate, 1g salt	Dairy free	**4**

Try Something Different

Replace the goat's cheese with two roasted, skinless chicken breasts, shredded.

Warm Spiced Rice Salad with Goat's Cheese

½ tbsp ground cumin

½ tsp ground cinnamon

2 tbsp sunflower oil

2 large red onions, sliced

250g (9oz) basmati rice

600ml (1 pint) hot vegetable or chicken stock

400g can lentils, drained and rinsed

For the salad

75g (3oz) watercress

250g (9oz) broccoli, steamed and chopped into 2.5cm (1in) pieces

25g (1oz) sultanas

75g (3oz) dried apricots, chopped

75g (3oz) mixed nuts and seeds

2 tbsp freshly chopped flat-leafed parsley

100g (3½oz) goat's cheese, crumbled

1 Put the cumin and cinnamon into a large deep frying pan and heat gently for 1–2 minutes. Add the oil and onions, then fry over a low heat for 8–10 minutes until the onion is soft and golden. Add the rice, toss to coat in the spices and onions, then add the stock. Cover and cook for 12–15 minutes until the stock is absorbed and the rice is cooked. Season, tip into a serving bowl and add the lentils.

2 To make the salad, add the watercress, broccoli, sultanas, apricots, and mixed nuts and seeds to the bowl. Scatter with the parsley, then toss together, top with the cheese and serve immediately.

Serves 4	EASY		NUTRITIONAL INFORMATION	
	Preparation Time 10 minutes	**Cooking Time** 20–30 minutes	**Per Serving** 700 calories, 27g fat (of which 6g saturates), 88g carbohydrate, 0.7g salt	Vegetarian Gluten free

Get Ahead

To prepare ahead Complete the recipe to the end of step 2 and store in an airtight container in the refrigerator for up to two days.
To use Complete the recipe.

Vietnamese Rice Salad

225g (8oz) mixed basmati and wild rice
1 large carrot, coarsely grated
1 large courgette, coarsely grated
1 red onion, finely sliced
4 tbsp roasted salted peanuts, lightly chopped
20g (³⁄₄oz) each fresh coriander, mint and basil, roughly chopped
100g (3¹⁄₂oz) wild rocket

For the Vietnamese dressing
2 tbsp light muscovado sugar
juice of 2 limes
4 tbsp fish sauce
6 tbsp rice wine vinegar or white wine vinegar
2 tbsp sunflower oil

1 Put the rice in a pan with 500ml (18fl oz) water. Cover, bring to the boil and cook for 20 minutes until the rice is just cooked. Tip on to a plastic tray, spread out and leave to cool.

2 Meanwhile, make the dressing. Put the sugar in a small pan and heat gently until it just begins to dissolve. Add the lime juice, fish sauce and vinegar. Stir over a low heat to dissolve the sugar. Take off the heat and add the oil. Stir into the rice with the carrot, courgette and onion.

3 Spoon the salad into a large bowl and top with peanuts, herbs and rocket. Cover and keep chilled.

A LITTLE EFFORT		NUTRITIONAL INFORMATION		Serves
Preparation Time 10 minutes	**Cooking Time** 20 minutes	**Per Serving** 279 calories, 9g fat (of which 1g saturates), 41g carbohydrate, 1g salt	Vegetarian Gluten free • Dairy free	**6**

Greek Pasta Salad

3 tbsp olive oil

2 tbsp lemon juice

150g (5oz) cooked pasta shapes, cooled

75g (3oz) feta cheese, crumbled

3 tomatoes, roughly chopped

2 tbsp small pitted black olives

½ cucumber, roughly chopped

1 small red onion, finely sliced

salt and ground black pepper

freshly chopped mint and lemon zest to garnish

1 Mix the oil and lemon juice together in a salad bowl, then add the pasta, feta cheese, tomatoes, olives, cucumber and onion.

2 Season with salt and pepper and stir to mix, then garnish with chopped mint and lemon zest and serve.

Serves 2	EASY		NUTRITIONAL INFORMATION	
	Preparation Time 10 minutes	**Cooking Time** 10–15 minutes	**Per Serving** 382 calories, 27g fat (of which 8g saturates), 25g carbohydrate, 2.5g salt	Vegetarian

Cook's Tip

Red bird's-eye chillies are always very hot. The smaller they are, the hotter they are.

200g (7oz) sugarsnap peas, trimmed

250g pack Thai stir-fry rice noodles

100g (3½oz) cashew nuts

300g (11oz) carrots, peeled and cut into batons

10 spring onions, sliced diagonally

300g (11oz) bean sprouts

20g (¾oz) fresh coriander, roughly chopped, plus coriander sprigs to garnish

1 red bird's-eye chilli, seeded and finely chopped (see page 40 and Cook's Tip)

2 tsp sweet chilli sauce

4 tbsp sesame oil

6 tbsp soy sauce

juice of 2 limes

salt and ground black pepper

Thai Noodle Salad

1 Bring a pan of salted water to the boil and blanch the sugarsnap peas for 2–3 minutes until just tender to the bite. Drain and refresh under cold water.

2 Put the noodles into a bowl, cover with boiling water and leave to soak for 4 minutes. Rinse under cold water and drain very well.

3 Toast the cashews in a dry frying pan until golden – about 5 minutes.

4 Put the sugarsnaps in a large glass serving bowl. Add the carrots, spring onions, bean sprouts, chopped coriander, chilli, cashews and noodles. Mix together the chilli sauce, sesame oil, soy sauce and lime juice and season well with salt and pepper. Pour over the salad, toss together, garnish with coriander sprigs and serve.

EASY		NUTRITIONAL INFORMATION		Serves
Preparation Time 20 minutes, plus 4 minutes soaking	**Cooking Time** 7–8 minutes	**Per Serving** 568 calories, 29g fat (of which 4g saturates), 65g carbohydrate, 2.9g salt	Gluten free Dairy free	**4**

2

Risotto

Risotto Milanese

50g (2oz) butter
1 onion, finely chopped
150ml (¼ pint) dry white wine
300g (11oz) arborio rice
1 litre (1¾ pints) chicken stock
large pinch of saffron strands
50g (2oz) Parmesan, freshly grated, plus shavings to serve
salt and ground black pepper

1 Melt half the butter in a heavy-based pan. Add the onion and cook gently for 5 minutes to soften, then add the wine and boil rapidly until almost totally reduced. Add the rice and cook, stirring, for 1 minute until the grains are coated with the butter and glossy.

2 Meanwhile, heat the stock in a separate pan to a steady, low simmer.

3 Add the saffron and a ladleful of the stock to the rice and simmer, stirring, until absorbed. Continue adding the stock, a ladleful at a time, until the rice is tender but still has some bite to it. This will take about 25 minutes and you may not need to add all the stock.

4 Add the remaining butter and the grated Parmesan. Season with salt and pepper to taste, garnish with shavings of Parmesan and serve.

Serves 4	EASY		NUTRITIONAL INFORMATION	
	Preparation Time 15 minutes	**Cooking Time** about 30 minutes	**Per Serving** 461 calories, 15g fat (of which 9g saturates), 64g carbohydrate, 0.6g salt	Gluten free

Prawn, Courgette and Leek Risotto

1 tbsp olive oil

25g (1oz) butter

1 leek, finely chopped

2 courgettes, thinly sliced

2 garlic cloves, crushed

350g (12oz) arborio rice

100ml (3½fl oz) dry white wine

1.6 litres (2¾ pints) vegetable stock

200g (7oz) cooked and peeled prawns

small bunch parsley or mint, or a mixture of both, chopped

salt and ground black pepper

1 Heat the oil and half the butter in a large shallow pan. Add the leek, courgettes and garlic and soften over a low heat. Add the rice and cook, stirring well, for 1 minute, then pour in the wine. Let bubble until the wine has evaporated.

2 Meanwhile, in another large pan, heat the stock to a steady, low simmer. Add a ladleful of the stock to the rice and simmer, stirring, until absorbed. Continue adding the stock, a ladleful at a time.

3 When nearly all the stock has been added and the rice is al dente (just tender but with a little bite at the centre), add the prawns. Season to taste and stir in the remaining stock and the rest of the butter. Stir through and take off the heat. Cover and leave to stand for a couple of minutes, then stir the chopped herbs through it. Serve immediately.

Serves 6	EASY		NUTRITIONAL INFORMATION	
	Preparation Time 10 minutes	**Cooking Time** 30 minutes	**Per Serving** 320 calories, 7g fat (of which 3g saturates), 49g carbohydrate, 1.3g salt	Gluten free

Tomato Risotto

1 large rosemary sprig

2 tbsp olive oil

1 small onion, finely chopped

350g (12oz) arborio rice

4 tbsp dry white wine

750ml (1¼ pints) hot vegetable stock

300g (11oz) cherry tomatoes, halved

salt and ground black pepper

shavings of Parmesan and extra virgin olive oil to serve

1 Pull the leaves from the rosemary and chop roughly. Set aside.

2 Heat the oil in a flameproof casserole, add the onion and cook for about 8–10 minutes until beginning to soften. Add the rice and stir to coat in the oil and onion. Pour in the wine, then the hot stock, stirring well to mix.

3 Bring to the boil, stirring, then cover and simmer for 5 minutes. Stir in the tomatoes and chopped rosemary. Simmer, covered, for a further 10–15 minutes until the rice is tender and most of the liquid has been absorbed. Season to taste.

4 Serve immediately with shavings of Parmesan and extra virgin olive oil to drizzle over.

EASY		NUTRITIONAL INFORMATION		Serves
Preparation Time 10 minutes	**Cooking Time** 25–30 minutes	**Per Serving** 264 calories, 4g fat (of which 1g saturates), 49g carbohydrate, 0.5g salt	Vegetarian Gluten free	**6**

Asparagus Risotto

50g (2oz) butter

2 shallots, diced

2 garlic cloves, crushed

225g (8oz) arborio rice

500ml (18fl oz) hot vegetable or chicken stock

2 tbsp mascarpone cheese

50g (2oz) Parmesan, finely grated, plus shavings to garnish

2 tbsp freshly chopped parsley

400g (14oz) asparagus spears, blanched and halved

salt and ground black pepper

1 Melt the butter in a heavy-based pan, add the shallots and garlic and cook over a gentle heat until soft.

2 Stir in the rice, cook for 1–2 minutes, then add the stock. Bring to the boil and simmer for 15–20 minutes, stirring occasionally to ensure that the rice isn't sticking, until almost all the stock has been absorbed and the rice is tender.

3 Add the mascarpone, half the grated Parmesan and half the parsley to the pan. Stir in the asparagus and the remaining parsley and Parmesan; season with salt and pepper. Divide the risotto among four plates, garnish with shavings of Parmesan and serve.

Serves 4	EASY		NUTRITIONAL INFORMATION	
	Preparation Time 10 minutes	**Cooking Time** 25 minutes	**Per Serving** 374 calories, 16g fat (of which 10g saturates), 47g carbohydrate, 1.1g salt	Gluten free

Cook's Tip

If you can't find pumpkin, use butternut squash.

Pumpkin Risotto with Hazelnut Butter

50g (2oz) butter

175g (6oz) onion, finely chopped

900g (2lb) pumpkin, halved, peeled, seeded and cut into small cubes (see Cook's Tip)

2 garlic cloves, crushed

225g (8oz) arborio rice

600ml (1 pint) hot chicken stock

grated zest of ½ orange

40g (1½oz) freshly shaved Parmesan

salt and ground black pepper

For the hazelnut butter

50g (2oz) hazelnuts

125g (4oz) butter, softened

2 tbsp freshly chopped flat-leafed parsley

1 To make the hazelnut butter, spread the hazelnuts on a baking sheet and toast under a hot grill until golden brown, turning frequently. Put the nuts in a clean teatowel and rub off the skins, then chop finely. Put the nuts, butter and parsley on a piece of non-stick baking parchment. Season with pepper and mix together. Mould into a sausage shape, twist the baking parchment at both ends and chill.

2 To make the risotto, melt the butter in a large pan and fry the onion until soft but not coloured. Add the pumpkin and sauté over a low heat for 5–8 minutes until just beginning to soften. Add the garlic and rice and stir until well mixed. Increase the heat to medium and add the stock a little at a time, allowing the rice to absorb the liquid after each addition. This should take about 25 minutes.

3 Stir in the orange zest and Parmesan, and season with salt and pepper. Serve the risotto with a slice of the hazelnut butter melting on top.

EASY		NUTRITIONAL INFORMATION		Serves
Preparation Time 15 minutes	**Cooking Time** 40 minutes	**Per Serving** 706 calories, 50g fat (of which 27g saturates), 51g carbohydrate, 1.1g salt	Gluten free	**4**

Garlic Risotto with Fresh Mussels

50g (2oz) butter
175g (6oz) onions, finely chopped
4 garlic cloves, crushed
225g (8oz) arborio rice
450ml (¾ pint) dry white wine
450ml (¾ pint) hot fish or vegetable stock
3 tbsp pesto
50g (2oz) Parmesan, freshly grated
4 tbsp freshly chopped parsley
1.4kg (3lb) fresh mussels in their shells, cleaned (see page 21)

1 Heat 25g (1oz) butter in a large pan. Add the onions and fry for about 5 minutes or until soft but not coloured. Add half the garlic and the rice and stir well.

2 Increase the heat to medium and add 300ml (½ pint) wine and the hot stock a little at a time, allowing the rice to absorb the liquid after each addition. This should take about 25 minutes.

3 Stir in the pesto, Parmesan and 2 tbsp chopped parsley. Keep the risotto warm.

4 Put the mussels in a large pan with the remaining butter, garlic and wine. Cover with a tight-fitting lid and cook for 3–5 minutes, shaking the pan frequently. Discard any mussels that do not open.

5 Spoon the risotto on to four serving plates. Pile the mussels on top, allowing the cooking juices to seep into the risotto, and scatter with the remaining chopped parsley.

Try Something Different

Replace the mussels with 350g (12oz) cooked, peeled prawns.

EASY		NUTRITIONAL INFORMATION		Serves
Preparation Time 10 minutes	**Cooking Time** 35 minutes	**Per Serving** 602 calories, 23g fat (of which 11g saturates), 49g carbohydrate, 1.3g salt	Gluten free	**4**

Cook's Tip

To enrich the flavour, add a splash of dry sherry or white wine to the pan when you add the rice.

Mushroom, Bacon and Leek Risotto

25g (1oz) dried mushrooms

250g (9oz) dry-cure smoked bacon, rind removed, chopped

3 leeks, chopped

300g (11oz) arborio rice

20g (3⁄4oz) chives, chopped

25g (1oz) freshly grated Parmesan, plus extra to serve

1 Put the mushrooms in a large heatproof bowl and pour in 1.4 litres (2½ pints) boiling water. Leave to soak for 10 minutes.

2 Meanwhile, fry the bacon and leeks in a large pan – no need to add oil – for 7–8 minutes until soft and golden.

3 Stir in the rice, cook for 1–2 minutes, then add the mushrooms and their soaking liquor. Cook at a gentle simmer, stirring occasionally, for 15–20 minutes until the rice is cooked and most of the liquid has been absorbed.

4 Stir in the chives and grated Parmesan, then sprinkle with extra Parmesan to serve.

Serves 4	EASY		NUTRITIONAL INFORMATION	
	Preparation Time 10 minutes	**Cooking Time** about 30 minutes	**Per Serving** 452 calories, 13g fat (of which 5g saturates), 62g carbohydrate, 2.6g salt	Gluten free

Try Something Different

Use turkey or veal escalopes instead of pork.

150g (5oz) Parma ham (6 slices)

6 thin pork escalopes, if necessary pounded with a rolling pin until wafer-thin

6 fresh basil leaves

25g (1oz) plain flour

about 75g (3oz) unsalted butter

175g (6oz) onions, finely chopped

2 garlic cloves, crushed

225g (8oz) arborio rice

450ml (¾ pint) dry white wine

450ml (¾ pint) hot chicken stock

3 tbsp pesto sauce

50g (2oz) Parmesan, freshly grated

4 tbsp freshly chopped flat-leafed parsley

salt and ground black pepper

Pork, Garlic and Basil Risotto

1 Preheat the oven to 180°C (160°C fan oven) mark 4. Lay a slice of Parma ham on each escalope and put a basil leaf on top. Fix in place with a wooden cocktail stick. Season and dip in the flour. Dust off any excess.

2 Melt a knob of the butter in a deep ovenproof pan. Fry the escalopes in batches for 2–3 minutes on each side until lightly golden. Melt a little butter for each batch. You will need about half the butter. Remove the escalopes, cover and keep warm in the oven.

3 Melt about another 25g (1oz) of the butter in the pan and fry the onions for about 10 minutes until soft and golden. Add the garlic and rice and stir well. Add the wine and stock. Bring to the boil, then put in the oven and cook, uncovered, for 20 minutes.

4 Stir in the pesto, Parmesan and parsley. Put the browned escalopes on to the rice, cover and put the pan back in the oven for a further 5 minutes or until the rice has completely absorbed the liquid and the escalopes are cooked through and piping hot.

EASY		NUTRITIONAL INFORMATION		Serves
Preparation Time 15 minutes	**Cooking Time** 50 minutes	**Per Serving** 431 calories, 18g fat (of which 6g saturates), 28g carbohydrate, 0.7g salt	Gluten free	**6**

Try Something Different

Instead of the squash, use 750g (1lb 11oz) peeled and seeded pumpkin.
Instead of the onion, use a fennel bulb.

Squash and Pancetta Risotto

125g (4oz) pancetta or smoked bacon, chopped

1 small butternut squash, peeled and cut into small chunks

1 onion, finely chopped

300g (11oz) arborio rice

1 litre (1¾ pints) hot vegetable stock

1 Put the pancetta or bacon and the butternut squash into a large deep frying pan and fry over a medium heat for 8–10 minutes.

2 When the pancetta is golden and the squash has softened, add the onion to the pan and continue to fry for 5 minutes until softened.

3 Stir in the rice, cook for 1–2 minutes, then add the stock. Bring to the boil and simmer for 15–20 minutes, stirring occasionally to ensure that the rice doesn't stick, until almost all the stock has been absorbed and the rice and squash are tender. Serve immediately.

Serves 4	EASY		NUTRITIONAL INFORMATION	
	Preparation Time 10 minutes	**Cooking Time** 40 minutes	**Per Serving** 390 calories, 9g fat (of which 3g saturates), 65g carbohydrate, 2g salt	Gluten free Dairy free

Wild Mushroom Risotto

6 tbsp olive oil

2 shallots, finely chopped

2 garlic cloves, finely chopped

2 tsp freshly chopped thyme, plus sprigs to garnish

1 tsp grated lemon zest

350g (12oz) arborio rice

150ml (¼ pint) dry white wine

900ml (1½ pints) vegetable stock

450g (1lb) mixed fresh mushrooms, such as oyster, shiitake and cep, sliced if large

1 tbsp freshly chopped flat-leafed parsley

salt and ground black pepper

1 Heat half the oil in a heavy-based pan. Add the shallots, garlic, chopped thyme and lemon zest and fry gently for 5 minutes or until the shallots are softened. Add the rice and stir for 1 minute until the grains are glossy. Add the wine, bring to the boil and let bubble until almost totally evaporated. Heat the stock in a separate pan to a steady, low simmer.

2 Gradually add the stock to the rice, a ladleful at a time, stirring with each addition and allowing it to be absorbed before adding more. Continue adding the stock slowly until the rice is tender. This should take about 25 minutes.

3 About 5 minutes before the rice is ready, heat the remaining oil in a large frying pan and stir-fry the mushrooms over a high heat for 4–5 minutes. Add to the rice with the parsley. The risotto should still be moist: if necessary add a little more stock. Check the seasoning and serve at once, garnished with thyme.

EASY		**NUTRITIONAL INFORMATION**		**Serves**
Preparation Time 10 minutes	**Cooking Time** 30 minutes	**Per Serving** 347 calories, 12g fat (of which 2g saturates), 50g carbohydrate	Vegetarian Gluten free	**6**

Risotto with Pancetta and Broad Beans

225g (8oz) podded fresh broad beans
50g (2oz) unsalted butter
1 tsp olive oil
125g (4oz) pancetta, chopped
1 onion, very finely chopped
about 1 litre (1¾ pints) vegetable stock
225g (8oz) arborio rice or carnaroli rice
150ml (¼ pint) dry white wine
2 tbsp freshly chopped flat-leafed parsley
1 tbsp freshly chopped tarragon
salt and ground black pepper
freshly shaved Parmesan to serve

1 Add the broad beans to a pan of lightly salted boiling water and cook for about 4 minutes until just tender. Drain and refresh under cold running water, then slip the beans out of their skins. Put the beans to one side.

2 Melt half the butter with the oil in a large pan. Add the pancetta and cook until golden, then add the onion and cook gently for 5 minutes or until softened and translucent, stirring from time to time. Meanwhile, bring the stock to a steady, low simmer in another pan.

3 Add the rice to the onion and stir well to ensure that all the grains are coated in butter. Pour in the wine and continue to stir over a low heat as it evaporates.

4 Add the stock a little at a time, allowing the rice to absorb the liquid after each addition. This should take about 25 minutes.

5 Remove from the heat and gently stir in the broad beans and remaining butter. Season with pepper and a little salt if needed, then stir in the parsley and tarragon. Serve immediately, topped with Parmesan.

Serves 4	EASY		NUTRITIONAL INFORMATION	
	Preparation Time 15 minutes	**Cooking Time** 35 minutes	**Per Serving** 466 calories, 19g fat (of which 9g saturates), 53g carbohydrate, 1.3g salt	Gluten free

Quick and Easy Pasta

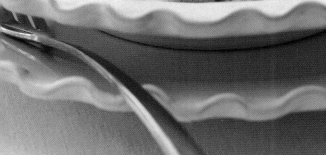

Pea, Mint and Ricotta Pasta

300g (11oz) farfalle pasta
200g (7oz) frozen peas
175g (6oz) ricotta
3 tbsp freshly chopped mint
2 tbsp extra virgin olive oil
salt and ground black pepper

1 Cook the pasta according to the packet instructions. Add the frozen peas for the last 4 minutes of cooking.

2 Drain the pasta and peas, reserving the water, then return to the pan. Stir in the ricotta and mint with a ladleful of pasta cooking water. Season well, drizzle with the olive oil and serve at once.

	EASY		NUTRITIONAL INFORMATION	
Serves **4**	**Preparation Time** 5 minutes	**Cooking Time** 10 minutes	**Per Serving** 431 calories, 14g fat (of which 5g saturates), 63g carbohydrate	Vegetarian

Cook's Tip

If cooking for vegetarians, omit the anchovies and serve with freshly grated Parmesan.

Ribbon Pasta with Courgettes and Capers

450g (1lb) dried pappardelle pasta
2 large courgettes, coarsely grated
50g can anchovies, drained and roughly chopped
1 red chilli, seeded and finely chopped (see page 40)
2 tbsp salted capers, rinsed
1 garlic clove, crushed
4 tbsp pitted black Kalamata olives, roughly chopped
4 tbsp extra virgin olive oil
2 tbsp freshly chopped flat-leafed parsley
salt and ground black pepper

1 Cook the pasta according to the packet instructions. About 1 minute before the end of the cooking time, add the courgettes, then simmer until the pasta is just cooked.

2 Meanwhile, put the anchovies into a small pan and add the chilli, capers, garlic, olives and oil. Stir over a low heat for 2–3 minutes.

3 Drain the pasta and put back in the pan. Pour the hot anchovy mixture on top, mix well and toss with the parsley. Season with salt and pepper and serve.

Serves 4	EASY		NUTRITIONAL INFORMATION	
	Preparation Time about 5 minutes	**Cooking Time** 8–10 minutes	**Per Serving** 557 calories, 18g fat (of which 2g saturates), 85g carbohydrate, 2.1g salt	Dairy free

Ham and Mushroom Pasta

350g (12oz) penne pasta
1 tbsp olive oil
2 shallots, sliced
200g (7oz) small button mushrooms
3 tbsp crème fraîche
125g (4oz) smoked ham, roughly chopped
2 tbsp freshly chopped flat-leafed parsley
salt and ground black pepper

1 Cook the pasta according to the packet instructions until al dente.

2 Meanwhile, heat the oil in a pan. Add the shallots and fry gently for 3 minutes until starting to soften. Add the mushrooms and fry for 5–6 minutes.

3 Drain the pasta, put back into the pan and add the shallots and mushrooms. Stir in the crème fraîche, ham and parsley. Toss everything together, season with salt and pepper and heat through to serve.

EASY		NUTRITIONAL INFORMATION	Serves
Preparation Time 5 minutes	**Cooking Time** 15 minutes	**Per Serving** 415 calories, 10g fat (of which 4g saturates), 67g carbohydrate, 1g salt	**4**

Kale, Anchovy and Crispy Breadcrumbs Pasta

75g (3oz) fresh breadcrumbs

300g (11oz) orecchiette or other shaped pasta

150g (5oz) kale, shredded

2 tbsp olive oil

1 red chilli, seeded and finely chopped (see page 40)

100g jar anchovies, drained and chopped

25g (1oz) Parmesan, freshly grated

1 Preheat the grill to medium and toast the breadcrumbs.

2 Cook the pasta according to the packet instructions until al dente. Add the kale to the pasta for the last 5–6 minutes of cooking time.

3 Heat 1 tbsp oil in a pan and fry the chilli and anchovies for 3–4 minutes.

4 Drain the pasta and kale, then tip back into the pan. Add the breadcrumbs, the anchovy mixture, the remaining oil and the Parmesan. Toss to mix, then serve.

Serves 4	EASY		NUTRITIONAL INFORMATION
	Preparation Time 5 minutes	**Cooking Time** 15 minutes	**Per Serving** 481 calories, 14g fat (of which 2g saturates), 72g carbohydrate, 3g salt

Try Something Different

Use rocket instead of spinach – no need to chop.

Pappardelle with Spinach

350g (12oz) pappardelle pasta

350g (12oz) baby leaf spinach, roughly chopped

2 tbsp olive oil

75g (3oz) ricotta

freshly grated nutmeg

salt and ground black pepper

1 Cook the pappardelle according to the packet instructions until al dente.

2 Drain the pasta well, return to the pan and add the spinach, oil and ricotta, tossing for 10–15 seconds or until the spinach has wilted. Season with a little freshly grated nutmeg and salt and pepper and serve.

EASY		NUTRITIONAL INFORMATION		Serves
Preparation Time 5 minutes	**Cooking Time** 8–10 minutes	**Per Serving** 404 calories, 11g fat (of which 3g saturates), 67g carbohydrate, 0.3g salt	Vegetarian	**4**

Spaghetti with Mussels

1kg (2lb) fresh mussels in their shells, cleaned (see page 21)

1kg (2lb) ripe, flavourful tomatoes, quartered

1 onion, chopped

4 garlic cloves

6 basil leaves, plus extra to garnish

150ml (¼ pint) white wine

400g (14oz) dried spaghetti

2 tbsp olive oil

2 red chillies, halved, seeded and chopped (see page 40)

salt and ground black pepper

1 Put the mussels into a large pan with a cupful of water. Cover with a tight-fitting lid and cook for 3–4 minutes, shaking the pan occasionally, until the mussels open. Using a slotted spoon, transfer the mussels to a bowl and discard any unopened ones.

2 Strain the mussel cooking juices through a muslin-lined sieve and set aside.

3 Put the tomatoes and onion into a shallow pan. Crush 2 garlic cloves and add them to the pan with the basil. Bring to the boil, then lower the heat and simmer for about 20 minutes until the tomatoes begin to disintegrate.

4 Press through a nylon sieve or mouli-légumes into a clean pan. Pour in the reserved mussel liquid and the wine. Bring to the boil and let bubble until reduced by half.

5 Cook the spaghetti according to the packet instructions until al dente.

6 Meanwhile, heat the oil in another pan. Chop the remaining garlic and add to the pan with the chillies. Cook until golden, then stir in the tomato sauce and mussels. Cover and simmer for 2–3 minutes until heated through. Season with salt and pepper to taste.

7 Drain the spaghetti, keeping 2 tbsp of the cooking water. Toss the spaghetti and reserved water with the mussel sauce. Serve immediately, garnished with basil.

EASY	NUTRITIONAL INFORMATION		Serves
Preparation Time 20 minutes	**Cooking Time** 35 minutes	**Per Serving** 530 calories, 10g fat (of which 1.5g saturates), 83g carbohydrate, 0.5g salt	Dairy free	**4**

Quick and Easy Carbonara

350g (12oz) tagliatelle
150g (5oz) smoked bacon, chopped
1 tbsp olive oil
2 large egg yolks
150ml (¼ pint) double cream
50g (2oz) Parmesan, freshly grated
2 tbsp freshly chopped parsley
salt and ground black pepper

1 Cook the pasta according to the packet instructions until al dente.

2 Meanwhile, fry the bacon in the oil for 4–5 minutes. Add to the drained pasta and keep hot.

3 Put the egg yolks in a bowl, add the cream and whisk together. Add to the pasta with the Parmesan and parsley and toss well. Season with salt and pepper and serve immediately.

	EASY		NUTRITIONAL INFORMATION
Serves 4	**Preparation Time** 5 minutes	**Cooking Time** 10 minutes	**Per Serving** 671 calories, 37g fat (of which 18g saturates), 66g carbohydrate, 1.8g salt

Pasta with Vegetables, Pinenuts and Pesto

300g (11oz) penne pasta

50g (2oz) pinenuts

1 tbsp olive oil

1 garlic clove, crushed

250g (9oz) closed cup mushrooms, sliced

2 courgettes, sliced

250g (9oz) cherry tomatoes

6 tbsp fresh pesto

25g (1oz) Parmesan, shaved

salt

1 Cook the pasta according to the packet instructions until al dente.

2 Meanwhile, gently toast the pinenuts in a frying pan, tossing them around until golden, then remove from the pan and set aside. Add the oil to the pan with the garlic, mushrooms and courgettes. Add a splash of water, then cover and cook for 4–5 minutes.

3 Uncover and add the tomatoes, then cook for a further 1–2 minutes. Drain the pasta and return to its pan. Add the vegetables, pinenuts and pesto to the drained pasta. Toss well to combine and serve immediately, with shavings of Parmesan.

EASY		NUTRITIONAL INFORMATION		Serves
Preparation Time 5 minutes	**Cooking Time** 10 minutes	**Per Serving** 567 calories, 29g fat (of which 5g saturates), 60.g carbohydrate, 0.4g salt	Vegetarian	**4**

Spiced Pork with Lemon Pasta

8 thick pork sausages
500g (1lb 2oz) dried pasta shells or other shapes
100ml (3½fl oz) dry white wine
grated zest of 1 lemon
juice of ½ lemon
large pinch of dried chilli flakes
300ml (½ pint) half-fat crème fraîche
2 tbsp freshly chopped flat-leafed parsley
25g (1oz) Parmesan, freshly grated
salt and ground black pepper

1 Remove the skin from the sausages and pinch the meat into small pieces. Heat a non-stick frying pan over a medium heat. When hot, add the sausagemeat and cook for 5 minutes, stirring occasionally, until cooked through and browned.

2 Meanwhile, cook the pasta according to the packet instructions until al dente.

3 Add the wine to the sausagemeat, bring to the boil and let bubble, stirring, for 2–3 minutes until the liquid has reduced right down. Add the lemon zest and juice, chilli flakes and crème fraîche. Season well with salt and pepper. Continue to cook for 3–4 minutes until reduced and thickened slightly.

4 Drain the pasta and return to the pan. Stir the parsley into the sauce and toss with the pasta. Serve immediately, with Parmesan.

	EASY		NUTRITIONAL INFORMATION
Serves 6	Preparation Time 10 minutes	Cooking Time 12 minutes	Per Serving 733 calories, 44g fat (of which 28g saturates), 71g carbohydrate, 1.8g salt

Pasta with Goat's Cheese and Sunblush Tomatoes

300g (11oz) conchiglie pasta
2 tbsp olive oil
1 red pepper, chopped
1 yellow pepper, chopped
½ tbsp sun-dried tomato paste
75g (3oz) sunblush tomatoes
75g (3oz) soft goat's cheese
2 tbsp freshly chopped parsley
salt

1 Cook the pasta according to the packet instructions until al dente.

2 Meanwhile, heat the oil in a pan and fry the red and yellow peppers for 5–7 minutes until softened and just beginning to brown. Add the tomato paste and cook for a further minute. Add a ladleful of pasta cooking water to the pan and simmer for 1–2 minutes to make a sauce.

3 Drain the pasta and return to the pan. Pour the sauce on top, then add the sunblush tomatoes, goat's cheese and parsley. Toss together until the cheese begins to melt, then serve.

Serves	EASY		NUTRITIONAL INFORMATION	
4	**Preparation Time** 5 minutes	**Cooking Time** 10 minutes	**Per Serving** 409 calories, 12g fat (of which 4g saturates), 64g carbohydrate, 0.4g salt	Vegetarian

Pasta with Chicken, Cream and Basil

1 tbsp olive oil

2 shallots, chopped

400g (14oz) chicken, cubed

125g (4oz) chestnut mushrooms, sliced

50g (2oz) sultanas

pinch of ground cinnamon

50ml (2fl oz) dry white wine

125ml (4fl oz) hot chicken stock

300g (11oz) farfalle pasta

142ml carton double cream

2 tsp Dijon mustard

2 tsp freshly chopped basil

salt

1 Heat the oil in a pan. Add the shallots and fry for 4–5 minutes. Add the chicken and cook until browned. Add the mushrooms and cook for 2 minutes. Stir in the sultanas and cinnamon.

2 Pour in the wine and stock and simmer for 12–15 minutes until the chicken is cooked.

3 Meanwhile, cook the pasta according to the packet instructions.

4 Stir the cream, mustard and basil into the chicken. Season with salt. Drain the pasta and return to the pan, then add the sauce, toss and serve.

EASY		NUTRITIONAL INFORMATION	Serves
Preparation Time 10 minutes	**Cooking Time** 25 minutes	**Per Serving** 612 calories, 27g fat (of which 12g saturates), 67g carbohydrate, 0.4g salt	4

Pasta with Leeks, Pancetta and Mushrooms

450g (1lb) dried conchiglie pasta
50g (2oz) butter
125g (4oz) pancetta, diced
2 medium leeks, thickly sliced
225g (8oz) chestnut mushrooms, sliced
1 garlic clove, crushed
150g pack soft herby cream cheese
salt and ground black pepper
basil leaves to garnish

1 Cook the pasta according to the packet instructions until al dente.

2 Meanwhile, melt the butter in a pan and add the pancetta, leeks, mushrooms and garlic. Cook over a medium heat for 5–10 minutes until the leeks are tender. Reduce the heat, add the cream cheese and season well with salt and pepper.

3 Drain the pasta, add to the sauce and toss well. Garnish with basil and serve.

EASY		NUTRITIONAL INFORMATION
Preparation Time 5 minutes	**Cooking Time** 15–20 minutes	**Per Serving** 765 calories, 39g fat (of which 22g saturates), 86g carbohydrate, 1.5g salt

Serves 4

300g (11oz) linguine pasta

2 tbsp olive oil

1 garlic clove, crushed

1 red chilli, seeded and finely chopped (see page 40)

4 tomatoes, seeded and chopped

900g (2lb) clams in their shells, washed and scrubbed

150ml (¼ pint) light dry white wine

2 tbsp freshly chopped parsley

Clams with Chilli

1 Cook the linguine according to the packet instructions.

2 Meanwhile, heat the oil in a large pan. Add the garlic, chilli and tomatoes and fry for 4 minutes, stirring gently. Add the clams and wine. Cover the pan with a lid and cook over a high heat for 3–4 minutes until the clam shells spring open – discard any that remain closed.

3 Drain the pasta, return to the pan, then add the clams with the sauce and the parsley. Toss together gently and serve immediately.

EASY		NUTRITIONAL INFORMATION		Serves
Preparation Time 15 minutes	**Cooking Time** about 10 minutes	**Per Serving** 405 calories, 8g fat (of which 1g saturates), 60g carbohydrate, 2.3g salt	Dairy free	**4**

Simple Salmon Pasta

500g (1lb 2oz) dried linguine pasta
a little olive oil
1 fat garlic clove, crushed
200ml (7fl oz) half-fat crème fraîche
225g (8oz) hot-smoked salmon, flaked
200g (7oz) peas
basil leaves to garnish
salt and ground black pepper

1 Cook the pasta according to the packet instructions, then drain, reserving a couple of tablespoons of the cooking water.

2 Meanwhile, heat the oil in a large pan, add the garlic and fry gently until golden. Add the crème fraîche, the flaked salmon and peas and stir in. Cook for 1–2 minutes until warmed through, then add the reserved water from the pasta.

3 Toss the pasta into the sauce, season with salt and pepper and serve immediately, garnished with basil.

Cook's Tip

Adding the reserved pasta cooking water stops the pasta absorbing too much of the crème fraîche.

EASY		NUTRITIONAL INFORMATION	Serves
Preparation Time 2 minutes	**Cooking Time** 10 minutes	**Per Serving** 630 calories, 13g fat (of which 6g saturates), 100g carbohydrate, 2.7g salt	**4**

Noodle and Rice Suppers

Chicken Chow Mein

Teriyaki Salmon with Spinach

Thai Noodles with Prawns

Prawn and Vegetable Pilau

Special Prawn Fried Rice

Turkey and Sesame Stir-fry with Noodles

Stir-fried Pork with Egg Noodles

Aubergine and Chickpea Pilaf

Prawns in Yellow Bean Sauce

Thai Egg Noodles

Marinated Pork with Vegetable Rice

Tuna with Coriander Rice

Rice and Red Pepper Stir-fry

Beef Chow Mein

Quick Pad Thai

Thai Noodles with Tofu

Coconut Fish Pilau

Crispy Noodles with Hot Sweet and
Sour Sauce

Chicken Chow Mein

250g (9oz) medium egg noodles

1 tbsp toasted sesame oil

2 skinless chicken breasts, cut into thin strips

1 bunch of spring onions, thinly sliced diagonally

150g (5oz) mangetouts, thickly sliced diagonally

125g (4oz) bean sprouts

100g (3½oz) cooked ham, shredded

120g sachet chow mein sauce

salt and ground black pepper

light soy sauce to serve

1 Cook the noodles in boiling water for 4 minutes or according to the packet instructions. Drain, rinse thoroughly in cold water, drain again and set aside.

2 Meanwhile, heat a wok or large frying pan until hot, then add the oil. Add the chicken and stir-fry over a high heat for 3–4 minutes until browned all over. Add the spring onions and mangetouts, stir-fry for 2 minutes, then stir in the bean sprouts and ham and cook for a further 2 minutes.

3 Add the drained noodles, then pour in the chow mein sauce and toss together to coat evenly. Stir-fry for 2 minutes or until piping hot. Season with salt and pepper and serve immediately with light soy sauce to drizzle over.

Serves 4	EASY		NUTRITIONAL INFORMATION	
	Preparation Time 10 minutes	**Cooking Time** 10 minutes	**Per Serving** 451 calories, 11g fat (of which 2g saturates), 59g carbohydrate, 1.3g salt	Dairy free

Cook's Tips

Furikake seasoning is a Japanese condiment consisting of sesame seeds and chopped dried seaweed; it can be found in supermarkets and Asian food shops.
Soba noodles are made from buckwheat and are gluten free. If you have a wheat allergy or gluten intolerance, check that the pack specifies '100% soba'.
Tamari is a wheat-free Japanese soy sauce.

Teriyaki Salmon with Spinach

550g (1¼lb) salmon fillet, cut into 1cm (½in) slices

3 tbsp teriyaki sauce

3 tbsp tamari (see Cook's Tips) or light soy sauce

2 tbsp vegetable oil

1 tbsp sesame oil

1 tbsp freshly chopped chives

2 tsp peeled and grated fresh root ginger

2 garlic cloves, crushed

350g (12oz) soba noodles (see Cook's Tips)

350g (12oz) baby spinach leaves

furikake seasoning (see Cook's Tips)

1 Gently mix the salmon slices with the teriyaki sauce, then cover, chill and leave to marinate for 1 hour.

2 Mix together the tamari or soy sauce, 1 tbsp vegetable oil, the sesame oil, chives, ginger and garlic. Set aside.

3 Cook the noodles according to the packet instructions. Drain and put to one side.

4 Heat the remaining vegetable oil in a wok or large frying pan. Remove the salmon from the marinade and add it to the pan. Cook over a high heat until it turns opaque – about 30 seconds. Remove from the pan and put to one side.

5 Add the drained noodles to the pan and stir until warmed through. Stir in the spinach and cook for 1–2 minutes until wilted. Add the soy sauce mixture and stir to combine. Divide the noodles among four deep bowls, then top with the salmon. Sprinkle with furikake seasoning and serve.

EASY		NUTRITIONAL INFORMATION		Serves
Preparation Time 10 minutes, plus 1 hour marinating	**Cooking Time** 6 minutes	**Per Serving** 672 calories, 30g fat (of which 4g saturates), 66g carbohydrate, 2.9g salt	Gluten free Dairy free	**4**

Thai Noodles with Prawns

4–6 tsp Thai red curry paste

175g (6oz) medium egg noodles (wholewheat if possible)

2 small red onions, chopped

1 lemongrass stalk, trimmed and sliced

1 fresh red bird's-eye chilli, seeded and finely chopped (see pages 40 and 47)

300ml (½ pint) reduced-fat coconut milk

400g (14oz) raw tiger prawns, peeled and deveined

4 tbsp freshly chopped coriander, plus extra freshly torn coriander to garnish

salt and ground black pepper

1 Put 2 litres (3½ pints) boiling water in a large pan. Add the curry paste, noodles, onions, lemongrass, chilli and coconut milk. Bring to the boil, then add the prawns and chopped coriander. Simmer for 2–3 minutes until the prawns turn pink. Season with salt and pepper. Divide the noodles among four large bowls and sprinkle with the torn coriander.

Cook's Tip

Don't overcook this dish or the noodles will be soggy and the prawns tough.

Serves	EASY		NUTRITIONAL INFORMATION	
4	**Preparation Time** 10 minutes	**Cooking Time** 5 minutes	**Per Serving** 343 calories, 11g fat (of which 2g saturates), 40g carbohydrate, 1g salt	Dairy free

Cook's Tip

The word 'pilau', or 'pilaf', comes from the Persian *pilaw*. The dish originated in the East and consists of rice flavoured with spices, to which vegetables, poultry, meat, fish or shellfish are added.

250g (9oz) long-grain rice

1 broccoli head, broken into florets

150g (5oz) baby sweetcorn, halved

200g (7oz) sugarsnap peas

1 red pepper, sliced into thin strips

400g (14oz) cooked and peeled king prawns

Prawn and Vegetable Pilau

For the dressing

1 tbsp sesame oil

5cm (2in) piece fresh root ginger, grated

juice of 1 lime

1–2 tbsp light soy sauce

1 Put the rice in a large wide pan – it needs to be really big, as you're cooking the rice and steaming the veg on top, then tossing it all together. Add 600ml (1 pint) boiling water. Cover, bring to the boil, then reduce the heat to low and cook the rice according to the packet instructions.

2 About 10 minutes before the end of the rice cooking time, add the broccoli, corn, sugarsnaps and red pepper. Stir well, then cover and cook until the vegetables and rice are just tender.

3 Meanwhile, put the prawns into a bowl. Add the sesame oil, ginger, lime and soy sauce. Mix the prawns and dressing into the cooked vegetables and rice and toss through well. Serve immediately.

Serves 4	EASY		NUTRITIONAL INFORMATION	
	Preparation Time 10 minutes	**Cooking Time** 15–20 minutes	**Per Serving** 360 calories, 5g fat (of which 1g saturates), 61g carbohydrate, 1.8g salt	Dairy free

Cook's Tips

Nasi goreng is a spicy Indonesian dish traditionally eaten for breakfast. Nasi goreng paste can be bought at large supermarkets and Asian food shops.
If you can't find microwave rice, use 200g (7oz) long-grain rice, cooked according to the packet instructions – but do not overcook. Rinse in cold water and drain well before you begin the recipe.

Special Prawn Fried Rice

1 tbsp sesame oil
6 tbsp nasi goreng paste (see Cook's Tips)
200g (7oz) green cabbage, shredded
250g (9oz) cooked and peeled large prawns
2 x 250g packs of microwave rice (see Cook's Tips)
2 tbsp light soy sauce
1 tbsp sunflower oil
2 medium eggs, beaten
2 spring onions, thinly sliced
1 lime, cut into wedges, to serve

1 Heat the sesame oil in a wok and fry the nasi goreng paste for 1–2 minutes. Add the cabbage and stir-fry for 2–3 minutes. Add the prawns and stir briefly, then add the rice and soy sauce and cook for a further 5 minutes, stirring occasionally.

2 To make the omelette, heat the sunflower oil in a non-stick frying pan (about 25.5cm/10in in diameter) and add the eggs. Swirl around to cover the base of the pan in a thin layer and cook for 2–3 minutes until set.

3 Roll up the omelette and cut it into strips. Serve the rice scattered with strips of omelette and spring onions and pass round the lime wedges to squeeze over.

EASY		NUTRITIONAL INFORMATION		Serves
Preparation Time 5 minutes	**Cooking Time** 10–15 minutes	**Per Serving** 412 calories, 18g fat (of which 3g saturates), 46g carbohydrate, 1.9g salt	Dairy free	**4**

Turkey and Sesame Stir-fry with Noodles

300g (11oz) turkey breast fillets, cut into thin strips

3 tbsp teriyaki marinade

3 tbsp clear honey

500g (1lb 2oz) medium egg noodles

about 1 tbsp sesame oil, plus extra for the noodles

300g (11oz) ready-prepared mixed stir-fry vegetables, such as carrots, broccoli, red cabbage, mangetouts, bean sprouts and purple spring onions

2 tbsp sesame seeds, lightly toasted in a dry wok or heavy-based pan

1 Put the turkey strips in a large bowl with the teriyaki marinade and honey and stir to coat. Cover and set aside for 5 minutes.

2 Bring a large pan of water to the boil and cook the noodles for about 4 minutes or according to the packet instructions. Drain well, then toss in a little sesame oil.

3 Heat 1 tbsp oil in a wok or large frying pan and add the turkey, reserving the marinade. Stir-fry over a very high heat for 2–3 minutes until cooked through and beginning to brown. Add a drop more oil, if needed, then add the vegetables and reserved marinade. Continue to cook over a high heat, stirring, until the vegetables have started to soften and the sauce is warmed through.

4 Serve immediately with the noodles, scattered with the sesame seeds.

EASY		NUTRITIONAL INFORMATION		Serves
Preparation Time 5 minutes, plus 5 minutes marinating	**Cooking Time** 10 minutes	**Per Serving** 672 calories, 18g fat (of which 4g saturates), 97g carbohydrate, 0.7g salt	Dairy free	**4**

Cook's Tip

Creamed coconut is a solid white block of coconut, which can be added directly in chunks to sauces or reconstituted with water.

Stir-fried Pork with Egg Noodles

150g (5oz) medium egg noodles
450g (1lb) pork escalope, cut into thin strips
2 tsp soy sauce
4–6 tbsp sunflower oil
125g (4oz) carrots, peeled and cut into matchsticks
225g (8oz) broccoli, cut into florets
150g (5oz) sugarsnap peas, halved diagonally
125g (4oz) mushrooms, thickly sliced
1 bunch of spring onions, thinly sliced
3 tbsp Thai green curry paste
150g (5oz) creamed coconut, roughly chopped and dissolved in 300ml (½ pint) boiling water (see Cook's Tip)
150ml (¼ pint) chicken stock
Thai fish sauce (optional)
salt and ground black pepper

1 Bring a pan of water to the boil and cook the noodles for 4 minutes or according to the packet instructions. Drain, then plunge into cold water. Set aside.

2 Season the pork with salt, pepper and soy sauce. Heat 1 tbsp oil in a wok or large frying pan. Fry the pork in two batches over a high heat, cooking each batch for 2–3 minutes until lightly browned and adding extra oil if necessary. Remove and set aside.

3 Heat 3 tbsp oil and stir-fry the carrots, broccoli and sugarsnap peas for 2–3 minutes. Add the mushrooms and spring onions, reserving a few to garnish, and fry for 1–2 minutes. Remove and set aside.

4 Add the curry paste, coconut and chicken stock to the pan. Bring to the boil and simmer for 5 minutes. Drain the noodles and add to the pan with the pork and vegetables. Stir well, bring to the boil and simmer for 1–2 minutes to heat through. Season with salt and pepper and a splash of fish sauce, if you like. Serve immediately, garnished with spring onions.

Serves 4	EASY		NUTRITIONAL INFORMATION	
	Preparation Time 15 minutes	**Cooking Time** 20 minutes	**Per Serving** 778 calories, 55g fat (of which 27g saturates), 37g carbohydrate, 1g salt	Dairy free

Get Ahead

To prepare ahead, fry the aubergine and onion as in step 1. Cover and keep in a cool place for up to 1½ hours. **To use** Complete the recipe.

4–6 tbsp olive oil

275g (10oz) aubergine, roughly chopped

225g (8oz) onions, finely chopped

25g (1oz) butter

½ tsp cumin seeds

175g (6oz) long-grain rice

600ml (1 pint) vegetable or chicken stock

400g can chickpeas, drained and rinsed

225g (8oz) baby spinach leaves

salt and ground black pepper

Aubergine and Chickpea Pilaf

1 Heat 2 tbsp oil in a large pan or flameproof casserole over a medium heat. Fry the aubergine for 4–5 minutes, in batches, until a deep golden brown, adding a little more oil if necessary. Remove from the pan with a slotted spoon and put to one side. Add the remaining oil to the pan. Cook the onions for 5 minutes, or until golden and soft.

2 Add the butter, then stir in the cumin seeds and rice. Fry for 1–2 minutes, pour in the stock, season with salt and pepper and bring to the boil. Reduce the heat, then simmer, uncovered, for 10–12 minutes until most of the liquid has evaporated and the rice is tender.

3 Remove the pan from the heat. Stir in the chickpeas, spinach and reserved aubergine. Cover with a tight-fitting lid and leave to stand for 5 minutes until the spinach has wilted and the chickpeas are heated through. Adjust the seasoning to taste. Fork through the rice grains to separate them and make the rice fluffy before serving.

EASY		NUTRITIONAL INFORMATION		Serves
Preparation Time 10 minutes	**Cooking Time** 20 minutes, plus 5 minutes standing	**Per Serving** 462 calories, 20g fat (of which 5g saturates), 58g carbohydrate, 0.9g salt	Gluten free	**4**

Try Something Different

Instead of prawns use skinless chicken breast, cut into thin strips.

Prawns in Yellow Bean Sauce

250g pack medium egg noodles

1 tbsp stir-fry oil or sesame oil

1 garlic clove, sliced

1 tsp peeled and grated fresh root ginger

1 bunch of spring onions, trimmed and each stem cut into four, lengthways

250g (9oz) frozen raw peeled tiger prawns, thawed

200g (7oz) pak choi, leaves separated and the white base cut into thick slices

160g jar Chinese yellow bean stir-fry sauce

1   Put the noodles in a bowl, pour 2 litres (3½ pints) boiling water over them and leave to soak for 4 minutes. Drain and set aside.

2   Heat the oil in a wok over a medium heat. Add the garlic and ginger and stir-fry for 30 seconds. Add the spring onions and prawns and cook for 2 minutes.

3   Add the chopped white part of the pak choi and the yellow bean sauce. Fill the empty sauce jar with boiling water and pour this into the wok, too.

4   Add the noodles to the pan and continue to cook for 1 minute, tossing every now and then to heat through. Finally, stir in the green pak choi leaves and serve immediately.

Serves	EASY		NUTRITIONAL INFORMATION	
4	**Preparation Time** 10 minutes, plus 4 minutes standing	**Cooking Time** 5 minutes	**Per Serving** 394 calories, 10g fat (of which 2g saturates), 59g carbohydrate, 0.9g salt	Dairy free

Thai Egg Noodles

1 lemongrass stalk, inner leaves only, finely chopped

100g (3½oz) medium egg noodles

100g (3½oz) sugarsnap peas, halved diagonally

4 tbsp vegetable oil

4 garlic cloves, crushed

3 large eggs, beaten

juice of 2 lemons

3 tbsp Thai fish sauce

2 tbsp light soy sauce

½ tsp caster sugar

50g (2oz) roasted salted peanuts

½ tsp chilli powder

12 spring onions, roughly chopped

150g (5oz) bean sprouts

2 tbsp freshly chopped coriander, plus extra to garnish

salt and ground black pepper

1 Put the lemongrass in a heatproof bowl with the noodles. Pour in 600ml (1 pint) boiling water and set aside for 20 minutes, stirring from time to time.

2 Cook the sugarsnap peas in salted boiling water for 1 minute, then drain and plunge them into ice-cold water.

3 Heat the oil in a wok or large frying pan, add the garlic and fry for 30 seconds. Add the beaten eggs and cook gently until lightly scrambled. Add the lemon juice, fish sauce, soy sauce, sugar, peanuts, chilli powder, spring onions and bean sprouts to the eggs. Pour the noodles, lemongrass and soaking liquid into the pan. Bring to the boil and bubble for 4–5 minutes, stirring from time to time.

4 Drain the sugarsnap peas, then add them to the noodle mixture with the chopped coriander. Heat through and season with salt and pepper. Garnish with coriander and serve immediately.

EASY		NUTRITIONAL INFORMATION		Serves
Preparation Time 15 minutes, plus 20 minutes soaking	**Cooking Time** 12–15 minutes	**Per Serving** 289 calories, 18g fat (of which 3g saturates), 24g carbohydrate, 2.9g salt	Dairy free	**4**

Marinated Pork with Vegetable Rice

1 tsp peeled and grated fresh root ginger

2 tbsp soy sauce

2 tbsp freshly chopped rosemary

4 rindless pork steaks

150g (5oz) brown rice

450ml (3/4 pint) hot vegetable stock

1 tbsp, plus 1 tsp olive oil

1 red onion, chopped

1 red pepper, chopped

a handful of shredded Savoy cabbage

1 Mix the ginger, soy sauce and rosemary in a shallow dish. Add the pork steaks, turn to coat, then set aside.

2 Put the rice in a pan and pour in the stock. Cover and bring to the boil, then simmer over a low heat for 20 minutes or until the rice is tender and the liquid has been absorbed.

3 Meanwhile, heat 1 tbsp oil in a frying pan. Add the onion, red pepper and cabbage and fry for 10 minutes. Heat 1 tsp oil in a separate frying pan and fry the steaks for 4–5 minutes on each side. Stir the vegetables through the rice, then serve with the pork.

Serves 4	EASY		NUTRITIONAL INFORMATION	
	Preparation Time 10 minutes	**Cooking Time** 20–25 minutes	**Per Serving** 462 calories, 11g fat (of which 4g saturates), 41g carbohydrate, 2.2g salt	Gluten free Dairy free

Tuna with Coriander Rice

250g (9oz) basmati rice

8 x 125g (4oz) tuna steaks

5cm (2in) piece fresh root ginger, peeled and grated

1 tbsp olive oil

100ml (3½fl oz) orange juice

300g (11oz) pak choi, roughly chopped

a small handful of freshly chopped coriander

ground black pepper

lime wedges to garnish

1 Cook the rice according to the packet instructions. Meanwhile, put the tuna steaks in a shallow dish. Add the ginger, oil and orange juice and season well with pepper. Turn the tuna over to coat.

2 Heat a non-stick frying pan until really hot. Add 4 tuna steaks and half the marinade. Cook for 1–2 minutes on each side until just cooked. Repeat with the remaining tuna and marinade. Remove the fish from the pan and keep warm.

3 Add the pak choi to the frying pan and cook for 1–2 minutes until wilted. When the rice is cooked, drain and stir the coriander through it. Serve the tuna with the pak choi, rice and pan juices and garnish with lime wedges.

Serves 4	EASY		NUTRITIONAL INFORMATION	
	Preparation Time 5 minutes	**Cooking Time** 10 minutes	**Per Serving** 451 calories, 10g fat (of which 2g saturates), 54g carbohydrate, 0.4g salt	Gluten free Dairy free

75g (3oz) long-grain rice

200ml (7fl oz) hot vegetable stock

2 tsp vegetable oil

½ onion, sliced

2 rashers streaky bacon

1 small red pepper, halved, seeded and cut into chunks

a handful of frozen peas

a dash of Worcestershire sauce

Rice and Red Pepper Stir-fry

1 Put the rice in a pan and pour in the hot stock. Cover, bring to the boil and simmer for 10 minutes until the rice is tender and the liquid has been absorbed.

2 Heat the oil in a frying pan over a medium heat. Add the onion and fry for 5 minutes, then add the bacon and red pepper. Fry for 5 minutes until the bacon is crisp. Stir in the cooked rice and the peas. Cook, stirring occasionally, for 2–3 minutes until the rice is hot and the peas are tender. Add a dash of Worcestershire sauce and serve.

EASY		NUTRITIONAL INFORMATION		Serves
Preparation Time 5 minutes	**Cooking Time** 15 minutes	**Per Serving** 584 calories, 20g fat (of which 5g saturates), 82g carbohydrate, 1.7g salt	Dairy free	**1**

2 tsp dark soy sauce

4 tsp dry sherry

1 tsp cornflour

1 tsp sugar

1 tbsp sesame oil

225g (8oz) rump steak, cut into thin strips about 7.5cm (3in) long

175g (6oz) egg noodles

3 tbsp vegetable oil

1 bunch of spring onions, sliced

3 garlic cloves, crushed

1 large green chilli, deseeded and sliced (see page 40)

125g (4oz) Chinese leaves, or cabbage, sliced

50g (2oz) bean sprouts

salt and ground black pepper

Beef Chow Mein

1 Put the soy sauce, sherry, cornflour, sugar and 1 tsp sesame oil in a bowl and whisk together. Pour this mixture over the beef. Cover and marinate in the refrigerator for at least 1 hour or overnight.

2 Cook the noodles for 4 minutes or according to the packet instructions. Rinse in cold water and drain.

3 Drain the beef, reserving the marinade. Heat the vegetable oil in a wok or large non-stick frying pan and fry the beef over a high heat until well browned. Remove with a slotted spoon and set aside.

4 Add the spring onions, garlic, chilli, Chinese leaves or cabbage and the bean sprouts to the pan and stir-fry for 2–3 minutes. Return the beef to the pan with the noodles and reserved marinade. Bring to the boil, stirring all the time, and bubble for 2–3 minutes. Sprinkle the remaining sesame oil over it, season with salt and pepper and serve immediately.

Serves 4	EASY		NUTRITIONAL INFORMATION	
	Preparation Time 15 minutes, plus marinating	**Cooking Time** 15 minutes	**Per Serving** 408 calories, 20g fat (of which 5g saturates), 38g carbohydrate, 1.2g salt	Dairy free

Cook's Tips

If you can't find satay and sweet chilli pesto, substitute 2 tbsp peanut butter and 1 tbsp sweet chilli sauce.

Chilli soy sauce can be replaced with 2 tbsp light soy sauce and ¹/₂ red chilli, finely chopped (see page 40).

Quick Pad Thai

250g (9oz) wide ribbon rice noodles

3 tbsp satay and sweet chilli pesto (see Cook's Tips)

125g (4oz) mangetouts, thinly sliced

125g (4oz) sugarsnap peas, thinly sliced

3 medium eggs, beaten

3 tbsp chilli soy sauce, plus extra to serve (see Cook's Tips)

250g (9oz) cooked and peeled tiger prawns

25g (1oz) dry-roasted peanuts, roughly crushed

lime wedges to serve (optional)

1 Put the noodles in a heatproof bowl, cover with boiling water and soak for 4 minutes until softened. Drain, rinse under cold water and set aside.

2 Heat a wok or large frying pan until hot, add the chilli pesto and stir-fry for 1 minute. Add the mangetouts and sugarsnap peas and cook for a further 2 minutes. Tip into a bowl. Put the pan back on the heat, add the eggs and cook, stirring, for 1 minute.

3 Add the soy sauce, prawns and noodles to the pan. Toss well and cook for 3 minutes until piping hot. Return the vegetables to the pan, cook for a further minute until heated through, then sprinkle with the peanuts. Serve with extra soy sauce and lime wedges to squeeze over it, if you like.

EASY		NUTRITIONAL INFORMATION		Serves
Preparation Time 12 minutes, plus 4 minutes soaking	**Cooking Time** 8 minutes	**Per Serving** 451 calories, 13g fat (of which 3g saturates), 56g carbohydrate, 2.6g salt	Dairy free	**4**

Thai Noodles with Tofu

125g (4oz) firm tofu, drained and cut into
2.5cm (1in) cubes

8 shallots, halved

1 garlic clove, crushed

2.5cm (1in) piece fresh root ginger, peeled and grated

2 tbsp soy sauce

1 tsp rice vinegar

225g (8oz) rice noodles

25g (1oz) unsalted peanuts

2 tbsp sunflower oil

15g (½oz) dried shrimps (optional)

1 medium egg, beaten

25g (1oz) bean sprouts

fresh basil leaves to garnish

For the sauce

1 dried red chilli, seeded and finely chopped

2 tbsp lemon juice

1 tbsp Thai fish sauce

1 tbsp caster sugar

2 tbsp smooth peanut butter

1 Preheat the oven to 200°C (180°C fan oven) mark 6. Put the tofu and shallots in a small roasting pan. Put the garlic, ginger, soy sauce, vinegar and 2 tbsp water in a bowl and stir well. Pour the mixture over the tofu and shallots and toss well to coat. Roast near the top of the oven for 30 minutes until the tofu and shallots are golden.

2 Meanwhile, soak the noodles according to the packet instructions. Drain and set aside. Toast the peanuts, then chop.

3 To make the sauce, put all the ingredients in a small pan and stir over a gentle heat until the sugar dissolves. Keep the sauce warm.

4 Heat the oil in a wok or large frying pan and stir-fry the dried shrimps, if using, for 1 minute. Add the drained noodles and beaten egg to the pan and stir over a medium heat for 3 minutes. Add the tofu and shallots, together with any pan juices. Stir well, then remove from the heat.

5 Stir in the bean sprouts and the sauce, then divide among four warmed serving plates. Sprinkle with the toasted peanuts and serve immediately, garnished with basil leaves.

EASY		NUTRITIONAL INFORMATION		Serves
Preparation Time 25 minutes	**Cooking Time** 35 minutes	**Per Serving** 431 calories, 15g fat (of which 3g saturates), 61g carbohydrate, 2.1g salt	Dairy free	**4**

Try Something Different

There are plenty of alternatives to cod: try coley (saithe), sea bass or pollack.

Coconut Fish Pilau

2 tsp olive oil

1 shallot, chopped

1 tbsp Thai green curry paste

225g (8oz) brown basmati rice

600ml (1 pint) hot fish or vegetable stock

150ml (¼ pint) reduced-fat coconut milk

350g (12oz) skinless cod fillet, cut into bite-sized pieces

350g (12oz) sugarsnap peas

125g (4oz) cooked and peeled prawns

25g (1oz) flaked almonds, toasted

squeeze of lemon juice

salt and ground black pepper

2 tbsp freshly chopped coriander to garnish

1 Heat the oil in a frying pan, add the shallot and 1 tbsp water and fry for 4–5 minutes until golden. Stir in the curry paste and cook for 1–2 minutes.

2 Add the rice, stock and coconut milk. Bring to the boil, then cover and simmer for 15–20 minutes until all the liquid has been absorbed.

3 Add the cod and cook for 3–5 minutes. Add the sugarsnap peas, prawns, almonds and lemon juice and stir over the heat for 3–4 minutes until heated through. Check the seasoning and serve immediately, garnished with coriander.

Serves 4	EASY		NUTRITIONAL INFORMATION	
	Preparation Time 15 minutes	**Cooking Time** 30 minutes	**Per Serving** 398 calories, 7g fat (of which 1g saturates), 53g carbohydrate, 0.4g salt	Gluten free Dairy free

Crispy Noodles with Hot Sweet and Sour Sauce

vegetable oil for deep-frying
125g (4oz) rice or egg noodles
frisée leaves to serve

For the sauce
2 tbsp vegetable oil
1 garlic clove, crushed
1cm (½in) piece fresh root ginger, peeled and grated
6 spring onions, sliced
½ red pepper, seeded and finely chopped
2 tbsp sugar
2 tbsp malt vinegar
2 tbsp tomato ketchup
2 tbsp dark soy sauce
2 tbsp dry sherry
1 tbsp cornflour
1 tbsp seeded and sliced green chillies (see page 40)

1 First, make the sauce. Heat the oil in a wok or large frying pan and stir-fry the garlic, ginger, spring onions and red pepper for 1 minute. Stir in the sugar, vinegar, ketchup, soy sauce and sherry. Blend the cornflour with 8 tbsp water and stir it into the sauce. Cook for 2 minutes, stirring. Add the chillies, cover and keep the sauce warm.

2 Heat the oil in a deep-fryer to 190°C (test by frying a small cube of bread; it should brown in 20 seconds). Divide the noodles into four portions and fry, a batch at a time, very briefly until lightly golden (take care as the hot oil rises up quickly).

3 Drain the noodles on kitchen paper and keep them warm while you cook the remainder.

4 Arrange the noodles on a bed of frisée leaves and serve immediately, with the sauce served separately.

A LITTLE EFFORT		NUTRITIONAL INFORMATION		Serves
Preparation Time 10 minutes	**Cooking Time** 15 minutes	**Per Serving** 317 calories, 14g fat (of which 2g saturates), 43g carbohydrate, 1.7g salt	Vegetarian Dairy free	**4**

5

Cooking for Friends

Cook's Tip

Ready-cooked mussels are available vacuum-packed from supermarkets. Alternatively, to cook from fresh, follow the preparation instructions on page 21, then put them in a large pan and add 50ml (2fl oz) water. Cover with a tight-fitting lid and cook for 3–4 minutes, shaking the pan occasionally, until the mussels open. Transfer to a bowl, discard any unopened mussels, and reserve the cooking liquid.

Simple Paella

1 litre (1³⁄₄ pints) chicken stock

¹⁄₂ tsp saffron

5 tbsp extra virgin olive oil

6 boneless, skinless chicken thighs, each cut into three pieces

1 large onion, chopped

4 large garlic cloves, crushed

1 tsp paprika

2 red peppers, seeded and sliced

400g can chopped tomatoes

350g (12oz) long-grain rice

200ml (7fl oz) dry sherry

500g (1lb 2oz) cooked mussels

200g (7oz) cooked and peeled tiger prawns

juice of ¹⁄₂ lemon

salt and ground black pepper

lemon wedges and fresh flat-leafed parsley to serve

1 Heat the stock, then add the saffron and leave to infuse for 30 minutes.

2 Heat half the oil in a frying pan and fry the chicken in batches for 3–5 minutes until golden brown. Set the chicken aside. Lower the heat slightly. Add the remaining oil. Fry the onion for 5 minutes or until soft. Add the garlic and paprika and stir for 1 minute. Add the chicken, red peppers and tomatoes. Stir in the rice. Add one-third of the stock and bring to the boil. Season with salt and pepper. Reduce the heat to a simmer. Cook, uncovered, stirring continuously, until most of the liquid has been absorbed.

3 Add the remaining stock a little at a time, letting the rice absorb it before adding more. (This should take about 25 minutes.) Add the sherry and cook for 2 minutes – the rice should be quite wet, as it will continue to absorb liquid. Add the mussels and prawns, with their juices, and the lemon juice. Stir in and cook for 5 minutes to heat through. Adjust the seasoning and serve with lemon wedges and parsley.

Serves	A LITTLE EFFORT		NUTRITIONAL INFORMATION
6	**Preparation Time** 15 minutes, plus infusing	**Cooking Time** 50 minutes	**Per Serving** 554 calories, 16g fat (of which 3g saturates), 58g carbohydrate, 0.5g salt

2 tbsp olive oil

1 onion, chopped

1 leek, chopped

2 tsp smoked paprika

2 tbsp tomato purée

450g (1lb) cod or haddock, roughly chopped

125g (4oz) basmati rice

175ml (6fl oz) dry white wine

450ml (³/₄ pint) hot fish stock

200g (7oz) cooked and peeled king prawns

a large handful of baby spinach leaves

crusty bread to serve

Fish Stew

1 Heat the oil in a large pan. Add the onion and leek and fry for 8–10 minutes until they start to soften. Add the smoked paprika and tomato purée and cook for 1–2 minutes.

2 Add the fish, rice, wine and stock. Bring to the boil, then cover and simmer for 10 minutes or until the fish is cooked through and the rice is tender. Add the prawns and cook for 1 minute until heated through. Stir in the spinach and serve with chunks of bread.

EASY		**NUTRITIONAL INFORMATION**		**Serves**
Preparation Time 15 minutes	**Cooking Time** about 30 minutes	**Per Serving** 347 calories, 7g fat (of which 1g saturates), 30g carbohydrate, 0.5g salt	Gluten free Dairy free	**4**

Cook's Tip

Oil-water spray is far lower in calories than oil alone and, as it sprays on thinly and evenly, you'll use less. Fill one-eighth of a travel-sized spray bottle with oil such as sunflower, light olive or vegetable (rapeseed) oil, then top up with water. To use, shake well before spraying.

Italian Meatballs

50g (2oz) fresh breadcrumbs
450g (1lb) minced lean pork
1 tsp fennel seeds, crushed
¼ tsp chilli flakes, or to taste
3 garlic cloves, crushed
4 tbsp freshly chopped flat-leafed parsley
3 tbsp red wine
oil-water spray (see Cook's Tip)
salt and ground black pepper
roughly chopped fresh oregano to garnish
spaghetti to serve

For the tomato sauce

oil-water spray (see Cook's Tip)
2 large shallots, finely chopped
3 pitted black olives, shredded
2 garlic cloves, crushed
2 pinches of chilli flakes
250ml (9fl oz) vegetable or chicken stock
500g carton passata
2 tbsp each freshly chopped flat-leafed parsley, basil and oregano

1 To make the tomato sauce, spray a pan with the oil-water spray and add the shallots. Cook gently for 5 minutes. Add the olives, garlic, chilli flakes and stock. Bring to the boil, cover and simmer for 3–4 minutes.

2 Uncover and simmer for 10 minutes or until the shallots and garlic are soft and the liquid syrupy. Stir in the passata and season with salt and pepper. Bring to the boil and simmer for 10–15 minutes, then stir in the herbs.

3 Meanwhile, put the breadcrumbs, pork, fennel seeds, chilli flakes, garlic, parsley and wine into a large bowl, season and mix together, using your hands, until thoroughly combined. (If you wish to check the seasoning, fry a little of the mixture, taste and adjust if necessary.)

4 With wet hands, roll the mixture into balls. Line a grill pan with foil, shiny-side up, and spray with the oil-water spray. Cook the meatballs under a preheated grill for 3–4 minutes on each side. Serve with the tomato sauce and spaghetti, garnished with oregano.

Serves 4	EASY		NUTRITIONAL INFORMATION	
	Preparation Time 15 minutes	**Cooking Time** 40 minutes	**Per Serving** 308 calories, 16g fat (of which 5g saturates), 16g carbohydrate, 1.2g salt	Dairy free

Pasta Shells Stuffed with Spinach and Ricotta

450g (1lb) fresh spinach, washed

125g (4oz) ricotta

1 medium egg

pinch of freshly grated nutmeg

grated zest of ½ lemon

50g (2oz) Parmesan, freshly grated

225g (8oz) conchiglione pasta shells

½ quantity of Classic Tomato Sauce (see page 13)

25g (1oz) pinenuts

salt and ground black pepper

1. Put the spinach in a large pan, cover and cook over a low to medium heat for 2–3 minutes until wilted. Drain and squeeze out the excess liquid. Chop finely.

2. Put the spinach into a large bowl with the ricotta and beat in the egg. Stir in the grated nutmeg, lemon zest and 25g (1oz) grated Parmesan. Season.

3. Preheat the oven to 200°C (180°C fan oven) mark 6. Meanwhile, cook the pasta according to the packet instructions for oven-baked dishes. Drain well.

4. Spread the Classic Tomato Sauce in the bottom of an 18 x 23cm (7 x 9in) ovenproof dish. Fill the shells with spinach mixture and arrange on top of the sauce. Sprinkle with the remaining Parmesan and the pinenuts. Cook in the oven for 20–25 minutes until golden.

Serves 6	EASY		NUTRITIONAL INFORMATION	
	Preparation Time 5 minutes	**Cooking Time** 30–35 minutes	**Per Serving** 293 calories, 13g fat (of which 5g saturates), 33g carbohydrate, 0.8g salt	Vegetarian

Try Something Different

Instead of salmon, use undyed smoked haddock fillet.

Salmon Kedgeree

50g (2oz) butter

700g (1½lb) onions, sliced

2 tsp garam masala

1 garlic clove, crushed

75g (3oz) split green lentils, soaked in 300ml (½ pint) boiling water for 15 minutes, then drained

750ml (1¼ pints) hot vegetable stock

225g (8oz) basmati rice

1 green chilli, seeded and finely chopped (see page 40)

350g (12oz) salmon fillet

salt and ground black pepper

1 Melt the butter in a flameproof casserole over a medium heat. Add the onions and cook for 5 minutes or until soft. Remove a third of the onions and put to one side. Increase the heat and cook the remaining onions for 10 minutes to caramelise. Remove and put to one side.

2 Put the first batch of onions back in the casserole, add the garam masala and garlic and cook, stirring, for 1 minute. Add the drained lentils and stock, cover and cook for 15 minutes. Add the rice and chilli and season with salt and pepper. Bring to the boil, cover and simmer for 5 minutes.

3 Put the salmon fillet on top of the rice, cover and continue to cook gently for 15 minutes or until the rice is cooked, the stock has been absorbed and the salmon is opaque.

4 Lift off the salmon and divide into flakes. Put it back in the casserole, and fork through the rice. Garnish with the reserved caramelised onion and serve.

EASY		NUTRITIONAL INFORMATION		Serves
Preparation Time 15 minutes, plus 15 minutes soaking	**Cooking Time** 55 minutes	**Per Serving** 490 calories, 15g fat (of which 2g saturates), 62g carbohydrate, 0.1g salt	Gluten free	**4**

Greek Pasta Bake

2 tbsp vegetable oil
1 onion, finely chopped
2 garlic cloves, crushed
450g (1lb) extra-lean minced lamb
2 tbsp tomato purée
400g can chopped tomatoes
2 bay leaves
150ml (¼ pint) hot beef stock
350g (12oz) dried macaroni
50g (2oz) Cheddar, grated
salt and ground black pepper

For the sauce

15g (½oz) butter
15g (½oz) plain flour
300ml (½ pint) milk
1 medium egg, beaten

1 Heat the oil in a large pan, add the onion and garlic and cook for 5 minutes to soften. Add the lamb and stir-fry over a high heat for 3–4 minutes until browned all over.

2 Stir in the tomato purée and cook for 1–2 minutes. Stir in the chopped tomatoes, bay leaves and hot stock and season with salt and pepper. Bring to the boil, lower the heat and cook for 35–40 minutes.

3 Meanwhile, make the sauce. Melt the butter in a small pan, then stir in the flour and cook over a medium heat for 1–2 minutes. Gradually add the milk, stirring constantly. Turn down the heat to low and cook, stirring, for 4–5 minutes. Remove from the heat and cool slightly. Stir in the beaten egg and season well with salt and pepper. Put to one side.

4 Cook the macaroni in a large pan of lightly salted boiling water according to the packet instructions until al dente.

5 Drain the pasta well and spoon half into a 2 litre (3½ pint) ovenproof dish. Spoon the meat mixture over it, then top with the remaining macaroni. Pour the sauce evenly over the top and scatter with the grated cheese. Cook at 180°C (160°C fan oven) mark 6 for 25–30 minutes until golden brown.

EASY		NUTRITIONAL INFORMATION	Serves
Preparation Time 10 minutes	**Cooking Time** about 1½ hours	**Per Serving** 736 calories, 30g fat (of which 13g saturates), 80g carbohydrate, 0.8g salt	**4**

Get Ahead

To prepare ahead Complete the recipe to the end of step 2, cool quickly, cover and chill for up to one day.
To use Bring back to the boil, stir in the pasta and complete the recipe.

Spicy Sausage and Pasta Supper

1 tbsp olive oil
200g (7oz) salami, sliced
225g (8oz) onion, finely chopped
50g (2oz) celery, finely chopped
2 garlic cloves, crushed
400g can pimientos, drained, rinsed and chopped
400g (14oz) passata or 400g can chopped tomatoes
125g (4oz) sun-dried tomatoes in oil, drained
600ml (1 pint) hot chicken or vegetable stock
300ml (½ pint) red wine
1 tbsp sugar
75g (3oz) dried pasta shapes
400g can borlotti beans, drained and rinsed
salt and ground black pepper
freshly chopped flat-leafed parsley to garnish
300ml (½ pint) soured cream and 175g (6oz) Parmesan, freshly grated, to serve

1 Heat the oil in a large pan over a medium heat and fry the salami for 5 minutes or until golden and crisp. Drain on kitchen paper.

2 Fry the onion and celery in the hot oil for 10 minutes or until soft and golden. Add the garlic and fry for 1 minute. Put the salami back in the pan with the pimientos, passata or chopped tomatoes, sun-dried tomatoes, stock, wine and sugar. Bring to the boil.

3 Stir in the pasta, bring back to the boil and cook for about 10 minutes, or according to the packet instructions, until the pasta is almost tender.

4 Stir in the beans and simmer for 3–4 minutes. Top up with more stock if the pasta is not tender when the liquid has been absorbed. Season with salt and pepper.

5 Ladle into warmed bowls and serve topped with soured cream and garnished with chopped parsley. Serve the grated Parmesan separately.

Serves 6	EASY		NUTRITIONAL INFORMATION
	Preparation Time 15 minutes	**Cooking Time** 30 minutes	**Per Serving** 629 calories, 39g fat (of which 18g saturates), 36g carbohydrate, 3.1g salt

1 half leg of lamb roasting joint, about 1.1kg (2½lb)

125g (4oz) smoked streaky bacon, chopped

150ml (¼ pint) red wine

400g can chopped tomatoes with chilli, or 400g (14oz) passata

75g (3oz) dried pasta shapes

12 sunblush tomatoes

150g (5oz) chargrilled artichokes in oil, drained and halved

basil leaves to garnish

Lamb and Pasta Pot

1 Preheat the oven to 200°C (180°C fan oven) mark 6. Put the lamb and bacon in a small, deep, flameproof roasting tin and fry for 5 minutes or until the lamb is brown all over and the bacon is beginning to crisp.

2 Remove the lamb and set aside. Pour the wine into the tin with the bacon – it should bubble immediately. Stir well, scraping the base to loosen any crusty bits, then leave to bubble until half the wine has evaporated. Stir in 300ml (½ pint) water and add the chopped tomatoes or passata, pasta and sunblush tomatoes.

3 Put the lamb on a rack over the roasting tin so that the juices drip into the pasta. Cook, uncovered, in the oven for about 35 minutes.

4 Stir the artichokes into the pasta and put everything back in the oven for 5 minutes or until the lamb is tender and the pasta cooked. Slice the lamb thickly. Serve with the pasta and scatter the basil on top.

EASY		NUTRITIONAL INFORMATION		Serves
Preparation Time 10 minutes	**Cooking Time** 50 minutes	**Per Serving** 686 calories, 36g fat (of which 16g saturates), 18g carbohydrate, 1.4g salt	Dairy free	**4**

Cook's Tip

Look out for bags of dried porcini pieces in supermarkets. These chopped dried mushrooms are ideal for adding a rich depth of flavour to stews or casseroles.

Italian Lamb Stew

2 half legs of lamb (knuckle ends)
2 tbsp olive oil
75g (3oz) butter
275g (10oz) onions, finely chopped
175g (6oz) carrots, finely chopped
175g (6oz) celery, finely chopped
2 tbsp dried porcini pieces (see Cook's Tip) or 125g (4oz) brown-cap mushrooms, finely chopped
9 pieces sun-dried tomato, finely chopped
150g (5oz) Italian-style spicy sausage or salami, thickly sliced
600ml (1 pint) red wine
400g (14oz) passata
600ml (1 pint) vegetable stock
125g (4oz) dried pasta shapes
15g (½oz) Parmesan, freshly grated
freshly chopped flat-leafed parsley to garnish

1 Preheat the oven to 240°C (220°C fan oven) mark 9. Put the lamb in a large roasting tin and drizzle 1 tbsp oil over it. Roast for 35 minutes.

2 Meanwhile, melt the butter with the remaining oil in a large flameproof casserole. Stir in the onions, carrots and celery and cook, stirring, for 10–15 minutes until golden and soft. Stir in the porcini pieces or mushrooms and cook for a further 2–3 minutes.

3 Add the sun-dried tomatoes, sausage, wine, passata and stock to the pan, then bring to the boil and simmer for 10 minutes.

4 Lift the lamb from the roasting tin, add to the tomato sauce and cover with a tight-fitting lid. Turn the oven down to 170°C (150°C fan oven) mark 3. Cook the stew for 3 hours or until the lamb is falling off the bone.

5 Lift the lamb from the casserole and put on to a deep, heatproof serving dish. Cover loosely with foil and keep warm in a low oven.

6 Put the casserole on the hob, stir in the pasta and bring back to the boil. Simmer for 10 minutes or until the pasta is tender. Stir in the Parmesan just before serving. Carve the lamb into large pieces and serve with the pasta sauce, garnished with parsley.

Serves	EASY		NUTRITIONAL INFORMATION
6	**Preparation Time** 35 minutes	**Cooking Time** 3¾ hours	**Per Serving** 610 calories, 34g fat (of which 16g saturates), 26g carbohydrate

Cook's Tip

If using 'no need to pre-cook' dried lasagne, add a little extra stock or water to the sauce.

1 quantity Bolognese Sauce (see page 13)

butter to grease

350g (12oz) fresh lasagne, or 225g (8oz) 'no need to pre-cook' dried lasagne (12–15 sheets)

3 tbsp freshly grated Parmesan

For the béchamel sauce

300ml (½ pint) semi-skimmed milk

1 onion slice

6 peppercorns

1 mace blade

1 bay leaf

15g (½oz) butter

15g (½oz) plain flour

freshly grated nutmeg

salt and ground black pepper

Classic Lasagne

1 To make the béchamel sauce, pour the milk into a pan and add the onion, peppercorns, mace and bay leaf. Bring almost to the boil, then remove from the heat, cover and leave to infuse for about 20 minutes. Strain. Melt the butter in a pan, stir in the flour and cook, stirring, for 1 minute until cooked but not coloured. Remove from the heat and gradually pour in the milk, whisking constantly. Season lightly with nutmeg, salt and pepper. Return to the heat and cook, stirring constantly, until the sauce is thickened and smooth. Simmer gently for 2 minutes.

2 Preheat the oven to 180°C (160°C fan oven) mark 4. Spoon one-third of the Bolognese sauce over the base of a greased 2.3 litre (4 pint) ovenproof dish. Cover with a layer of lasagne sheets, then a layer of béchamel. Repeat these layers twice more, finishing with a layer of béchamel to cover the lasagne.

3 Sprinkle the Parmesan over the top and stand the dish on a baking sheet. Cook for 45 minutes or until well browned and bubbling.

	EASY		NUTRITIONAL INFORMATION
Serves **6**	**Preparation Time** about 1 hour	**Cooking Time** 45 minutes	**Per Serving** 326 calories, 13g fat (of which 6g saturates), 37g carbohydrate, 0.5g salt

Butternut Squash and Spinach Lasagne

1 butternut squash, peeled, halved, seeded and cut into 3cm (1¼in) cubes

2 tbsp olive oil

1 onion, sliced

25g (1oz) butter

25g (1oz) plain flour

600ml (1 pint) milk

250g (9oz) ricotta cheese

1 tsp freshly grated nutmeg

225g bag baby leaf spinach

6 'no need to pre-cook' lasagne sheets

50g (2oz) pecorino cheese or Parmesan, freshly grated

salt and ground black pepper

1 Preheat the oven to 200°C (180°C fan oven) mark 6. Put the squash in a roasting tin with the oil, onion and 1 tbsp water. Mix well and season with salt and pepper. Roast for 25 minutes, tossing halfway through.

2 To make the sauce, melt the butter in a pan, then stir in the flour and cook over a medium heat for 1–2 minutes. Gradually add the milk, stirring constantly. Reduce the heat to a simmer and cook, stirring, for 5 minutes or until the sauce has thickened. Crumble the ricotta into the sauce and add the nutmeg. Mix together thoroughly and season with salt and pepper.

3 Heat 1 tbsp water in a pan. Add the spinach, cover and cook until just wilted. Season generously.

4 Spoon the squash mixture into a 1.7 litre (3 pint) ovenproof dish. Layer the spinach on top, then cover with a third of the sauce, then the lasagne. Spoon the remaining sauce on top, season and sprinkle with the grated cheese. Cook for 30–35 minutes until the cheese topping is golden and the pasta is cooked.

EASY		NUTRITIONAL INFORMATION		Serves 6
Preparation Time 30 minutes	**Cooking Time** about 1 hour	**Per Serving** 273 calories, 17g fat (of which 7g saturates), 18g carbohydrate, 0.6g salt	Vegetarian	

Cook's Tip

To save time, you can buy ready-to-use cannelloni tubes instead of using lasagne.

Cannelloni with Roasted Garlic

20 garlic cloves, unpeeled

2 tbsp extra virgin olive oil

15g (½oz) dried porcini mushrooms, soaked for 20 minutes in 150ml (¼ pint) boiling water

5 shallots or button onions, finely chopped

700g (1½lb) lean minced meat

175ml (6fl oz) red wine

2 tbsp freshly chopped thyme

about 12 lasagne sheets (see Cook's Tip)

142ml carton single cream

2 tbsp sun-dried tomato paste

butter to grease

75g (3oz) Gruyère cheese, finely grated

salt and ground black pepper

1 Preheat the oven to 180°C (160°C fan oven) mark 4. Put the garlic in a small roasting tin with 1 tbsp oil. Toss to coat the garlic in the oil and cook for 25 minutes or until soft. Leave to cool.

2 Meanwhile, drain the porcini mushrooms, putting the liquor to one side, then rinse to remove any grit. Chop the mushrooms finely.

3 Heat the remaining oil in a pan. Add the shallots and cook over a medium heat for 5 minutes until soft. Increase the heat and stir in the meat. Cook, stirring frequently, until browned. Add the wine, mushrooms, with their liquor, and thyme. Cook over a medium heat for 15–20 minutes until the liquid has almost evaporated. The mixture should be quite moist.

4 Peel the garlic cloves and mash them to a rough paste with a fork. Stir into the meat mixture, then season with salt and pepper and set aside.

5 Cook the lasagne according to the packet instructions until al dente. Drain, rinse with cold water and drain again.

6 Lay out each lasagne sheet on a clean teatowel. Spoon the meat mixture along one long edge and roll up to enclose the filling. Cut the tubes in half.

7 Mix the cream and sun-dried tomato paste together in a small bowl, then season with pepper. Preheat the oven to 200°C (180°C fan oven) mark 6 and grease a shallow baking dish.

8 Arrange a layer of filled tubes in the base of the baking dish. Spoon half the tomato cream over them and sprinkle with half the cheese. Arrange the remaining tubes on top and cover with the remaining tomato cream and cheese.

9 Cover the dish with foil and cook in the oven for 10 minutes. Uncover and cook for a further 5–10 minutes until lightly browned. Serve immediately.

A LITTLE EFFORT		NUTRITIONAL INFORMATION	Serves
Preparation Time 40 minutes	**Cooking Time** about 1 hour	**Per Serving** 430 calories, 20g fat (of which 9g saturates), 29g carbohydrate, 0g salt	**6**

Jambalaya

2 tbsp olive oil

300g (11oz) boneless, skinless chicken thighs, cut into chunks

75g (3oz) French sausage, such as saucisse sèche, chopped

2 celery sticks, chopped

1 large onion, finely chopped

225g (8oz) long-grain rice

1 tbsp tomato purée

2 tsp Cajun spice mix

500ml (18fl oz) hot chicken stock

1 bay leaf

4 large tomatoes, roughly chopped

200g (7oz) raw tiger prawns, peeled and deveined

1 Heat 1 tbsp oil in a large pan and fry the chicken and sausage over a medium heat until browned. Remove with a slotted spoon and set aside.

2 Add the remaining oil to the pan with the celery and onion. Fry gently for 15 minutes until the vegetables are softened but not coloured. Tip in the rice and stir for 1 minute to coat in the oil. Add the tomato purée and spice mix and cook for another 2 minutes.

3 Pour in the hot stock and return the browned chicken and sausage to the pan with the bay leaf and tomatoes. Simmer for about 20–25 minutes until the stock has been fully absorbed and the rice is cooked.

4 Stir in the prawns and cover the pan. Leave to stand for 10 minutes until the prawns have turned pink. Serve immediately.

Serves 4	EASY		NUTRITIONAL INFORMATION	
	Preparation Time 15 minutes	**Cooking Time** about 50 minutes, plus standing	**Per Serving** 558 calories, 25g fat (of which 6g saturates), 49g carbohydrate, 00g salt	Gluten free Dairy free

Index